*To my friends in the Churches' Fellowship
for Psychical and Spiritual Studies*

LIFE UNLIMITED

The Persistence of Personality Beyond Death

Allan Barham

VOLTURNA PRESS

ISBN: 0 85606 055 0

Published by Volturna Press, Hythe, Kent.

First published   October 1982

Typeset in 11 on 13pt Baskerville

by David J. Ellis

Fernwood, Nightingales, West Chiltington,
PULBOROUGH, West Sussex. RH20 2QT

Printed and bound in England by
Billing & Sons Limited
Worcester

Contents

Preface

By Arthur J. Ellison, D.Sc.(Eng.), C.Eng., F.I.Mech.E., F.I.E.E., Sen.Mem.I.E.E.E., Professor of Electrical Engineering at The City University; President of the Society for Psychical Research

It is a pleasure to write this preface to the second of Allan Barham's books on his experiences of psychical matters and his reflections about them. While the first book, *Strange to Relate*, was primarily concerned with his extensive personal experiences, this second book, which seems a worthy successor to the other, gives his opinions on various other matters of interest in the field of psychical research.

At our present state of knowledge, reliable explanations of all the facts Mr. Barham relates are not available. Scientific 'knowledge' does not cover much of the psychic, as yet. I pointed out the particular difficulties in this area of discourse in the earlier preface, and the author of this book is of course aware of these difficulties. To the naïve the explanations may be considered obvious—all of them (or nearly all) based on a 'next world' approach involving the so-called discarnate. To the more sophisticated, especially if they are familiar with modern work on the unconscious mind, the difficulties in the simple explanations are very obvious.

Perhaps one day we shall have a theory acceptable to all: but that day is not yet. At present we are still collecting facts and producing hypotheses (and many useful ideas are to be found in the vast literature of the East).

I wish the book a wide and thoughtful readership.

Beckenham,
Kent.
1981
           Arthur J. Ellison

Foreword

*By Ian Parrott, M.A., D.Mus., F.T.C.L., A.R.C.O., F.R.S.A.,
Professor of Music at the University College of Wales,
Aberystwyth; member of the Society for Psychical Research.*

Modern Western civilisation, no less than the Eastern bloc, is basically materialist in its outlook. The 'Third World'—the rest of mankind—continues to believe in spirits and in the reality of an unseen world, and is looked down upon by the Western and Eastern blocs as primitive and ignorant. This attitude has puzzled me for a long time. And so I welcome with considerable enthusiasm a book which rehabilitates the sensible views of the majority of mankind.

Moreover, it deals not with any of these three districts of the 'real' physical world, but acts as an eminently readable travellers' guide to the 'other' world. This is the world of Eternity, which Blake has described as 'the divine bosom into which we shall go after the death of the vegetated body'.

The present author calls it 'another sphere of life', and I would be inclined to describe it as 'another dimension'. It is *not* another part of the physical world, which materialists think is all there is. The Lambeth Conference of 1920 (referred to by the author) calls it 'behind and beyond', but something within us puts us in contact with it.

And this, basically, is the subject of the present book—a book which is partly autobiographical, telling of the pilgrimage which has led Allan and Janet to Canterbury, though they have not been quite like the Canterbury pilgrims of old.

My own attraction to the subject, as a professional musician, has been towards the paranormal music which Miss Jourdain heard at Versailles in 1902, and towards the products of the musical medium, Rosemary Brown, during the sixties and seventies.

I am thus particularly pleased that the first chapter is about *The Boy Who Saw True,* since the introduction to that convincing book was supplied by the composer, Cyril Scott.

Allan Barham takes the reader from the boy who saw further than his nose to Grace Rosher, who wrote with more wisdom than she knew. Then, although he devotes the following chapters to much that comes out of the séance room, he presents the balanced view of one who is *not* a Spiritualist. Indeed, his cautious view of extra-sensory perception has taken him, via the Society for Psychical Research, to the more recently established Churches' Fellowship for Psychical and Spiritual Studies. In 1974 he became the Chairman of its Psychic Phenomena Committee.

In steering away from the Spiritualists (who need no proof of a future life), the author gives us much valuable information on the attitudes of some churchmen (who have fought shy of adding knowledge to faith). But Allan Barham is, in the best sense of the phrase, 'a religious man'. The last chapter of the book is devoted to Divine Healing, and much wisdom is shown about the strange and improbable Universe in which we live—both here and there and beyond.

ONE

The Boy Who Saw True

By the time I began to take an interest in psychical study I had been a clergyman of the Church of England for fifteen years. But during that time the idea that psychical research might have some relevance to religion had never entered my mind.

There had, indeed, been an incident when my mother-in-law, while she was unconscious during an illness, seemed to have had what is called an out-of-the-body experience. In the course of this, she said, she had seen her little son and his uncle, both of whom had died some months earlier. Moreover, she had witnessed their meeting with two friends who, she learned later, had died unexpectedly during her period of unconsciousness. This had strengthened her conviction that life continued after death.

My mother-in-law was a staunch supporter of the Anglican Church—her husband was a churchwarden—and I never made any connection between her experience and psychic phenomena, which at that time I associated exclusively with Spiritualism.

Later on, I came to realise that when one came to know people really well, and questioned them about strange experiences they might have had, quite often they would tell me that, once or twice during their lives, they had heard or seen something which they could not explain.

As an example of this, the vicar of a parish near to mine told me that once, when he was alone in his church, he looked round and saw a man, whom he described in some detail, looking at an old photograph of the church that was hanging on a wall. He assumed this man was a casual visitor, but then, as he looked again, the man had disappeared—and if he had gone out by the door the vicar must have seen him do so. My friend, who certainly was no Spiritualist, simply took the view that the man had been a parishioner of an earlier period who had come to have a look at his former place of worship. The word, 'psychic', was never mentioned. Strange things happened from time to time, and that was that!

Nowadays some of the clergy have become rather materialistic in their religious outlook, and are sceptical about any meaningful life beyond death. They would probably explain away the two incidents I have just mentioned as tricks of the imagination.

But theological thinking was much more positive when I began my ministry, and I was so convinced that every human individual was a spiritual being with an eternal destiny that I never questioned it. What that destiny might be had not been a subject of study while I was preparing for my theological degree and, so far as I can remember, I never speculated about it.

One reason why Christian theology did not greatly concern itself with what was the nature of life after death was that the Bible appeared to speak with an uncertain voice on this subject. For instance, although Jesus is reported as saying on the cross to the repentant thief, "Today shalt thou be with me in paradise", St. Paul, on the other hand, taught that Christians after death will "sleep" until the Last Trump, when "the dead shall be raised incorruptible" (1 Corinthians 15.52). It is not surprising that the Church is confused about this subject. It is not to be wondered that many mourners have no conviction that those who have died are experiencing any kind of active life in which they will join them after their own death. I have been referring to those with religious faith. Agnostics and atheists do not, of course, have a conviction of any kind of life following death.

Psychic evidence would seem to agree neither with the usual Christian conception of an afterlife nor with the materialists' rejection of it. But, the Christians and others may well say, this psychic evidence comes through mediums, and no reliance can be placed on people like these. I shall have a good deal to say about mediums later on, but first

I should like to refer to some evidence of a psychic kind which came through someone who certainly would not be characterised by most people as a medium.

My mother-in-law and the vicar I have mentioned were not mediums, nor were the many others who very occasionally have had similar strange experiences which might be described as psychic; but more impressive than their evidence for a post-mortem life is that produced by a young boy whose diary was published in 1953 under the name of *The Boy Who Saw True* by Neville Spearman, to whom I am grateful for allowing me to quote from this remarkable book.

This was one of the first books on psychic subjects which I read when I became interested in psychical study. The diary is anonymous, and this fact might have detracted from its significance for me had not the Rev. Maurice Elliott, the Secretary of the Churches' Fellowship for Psychical Study, told me that he had known the author and could vouch for the authenticity of the diary.

By the time of the publication of the book, the writer of the diary had died, as he had not permitted his diary to be published during his lifetime. He was born in the eighteen seventies, and when he began writing the diary in 1885 it is clear that he knew nothing of Spiritualism. His family were strongly opposed to anything of a psychic nature, and believed that his experiences were simply childish fancies.

He was a precocious boy and would read adult books from his father's library, but from the contents of the diary it is obvious that they had contained nothing which helped him to understand the experiences which he, for some time at least, thought of as natural and shared by everybody, but which were in fact examples of an unusual gift of clairvoyance. The punctuation of the diary has been improved and there have been some spelling corrections. Also, most of the names were altered to avoid possible embarrassment among surviving relations and friends.

The diary begins on January 1st, 1885, but not until February 19th was there any reference to a psychic experience.

"... I saw Uncle Willie sitting in papa's chair, and smiling at us. And just then papa came back from bizzness, and after he had kissed us all, was going to sit down, when I cried 'Don't sit there, Uncle Willie is sitting in that chair.' And mamma looked all funny, and said, 'I rarely don't know what we're going to do with that child', and papa said, very cross, 'What *are* you talking about, boy? Why, your Uncle Willie has been dead these two years.' .... After I was in bed, mamma came up, like she always does, to give me my hug, and said she wanted to talk to me very seriously. So she sat down, and said that naughty little boys who told such dreadful wicked stories like that about poor Uncle Willie would never go to heaven, and I must promise never never to say such things again. Then I began to cry, and said it *wasn't* a story, and I *had* seen Uncle Willie, and that it'ud be a wicked story if I said I hadn't."

It is clear that the diarist had no idea that he had seen Uncle Willie clairvoyantly, and he couldn't understand why the rest of the family had not seen him. The child was very unhappy at school, apparently because of the excessive severity of his school-mistress. The doctor advised his parents to remove him from the school, which they did, and they engaged a tutor, Mr. Patmore. This change was an important turning point in the boy's life as the tutor proved sympathetic to his psychic experiences in a way that his parents certainly had not.

On July 20th, 1886, Grandpa appeared clairvoyantly and informed him that:—

"... heaven isn't a bit like what people think, and it's much nicer. He told me that by and by crowds of people will believe in the spirits, something like they believe in Jesus now, and they'll all be much happier and won't mind such a lot about death. I asked him if people stayed old in heaven when they had died old? And he laughed and said, no. He told me that where he was, people could make themselves look just as they wanted to look. If they like to think of themselves looking young, they look young, and the other way round too. He says he makes himself look old when he comes to see me, because if he didn't I wouldn't be able to know him. Though Arnold [a friend] doesn't jeer at me for seeing things, he said one day, 'If ghosts are supposed to be the spirits of dead people, why do they have clothes on, because clothes can't have spirits?' So I thought I'd ask Grandpa why he wasn't naked, or why all spirits aren't naked. And this seemed to tickle him a lot. But I couldn't catch him out, he is too sharp. He said, 'Do *you* think of yourself as going about naked?' So I said, 'No, I didn't.' Then he said, 'Well, neither do we. I have just told you, my lad, that we look as we think of ourselves. That is why people over here wear such a lot of different sorts of clothes, and why even I wear clothes that aren't the fashion any more with you in your world.'"

Mr. Patmore soon became intrigued with the boy's clairvoyance, as the following extract from the entry for August 24th shows:—

"Yesterday after dinner I saw a man in the room, and we had great fun with him. When I told Mr. Patmore he was there, he said, 'Let's ask him what he wants,' and he got his pencil ready to put it all down in short hand which he can do a bit. So to-day he gave me what he'd written for dictation lesson to put in my diary. It will be grand when it's all printed like Mr. Pepys, though I shall have to wait till I'm old, because of course mamma would kick up an awful rumpus if she saw it . . . .

"The first thing he [the spirit] said was 'Hello, Patmore. Fancy seeing you here.' Then Mr. P. asked who he was. And he said, 'What a question!' and that his name was Jimmy Cliff, and he was surprised that

Mr. P. didn't recognise him. So Mr. P. was very surprised too, and said he was blowed, but that of course he couldn't recognise him, because he couldn't see people who were dead, though I think he said another word. And now I'll write what Mr. P. gave me for dictation, which was quite easy because Mr. Cliff didn't use such long words as grandpa. Mr. Patmore says that I can put P. for Patmore and C. for Cliff if I like, to save time. So that is what I shall do, though it won't look very nice without the misters.

C.   What are you writing there?

P.   I'm writing down what you say.

C.   What the devil for?

P.   Because I want to remember what you tell us.

C.   What nonsense.

P.   Not at all, I'm interested. I'm very pleased you have come. But what gave you the idea?

C.   I like the place, and wanted to see it again. It was I who told you about these rooms. [The boy was on holiday in Harlech with Mr. and Mrs. Patmore.]

P.   Yes, I know you did. Tell me, how are you feeling?

C.   I never felt better in my life physically, but mentally—well, I seem to be a bit confused. It's damn queer.

P.   You used to be an Agnostic. I suppose you've altered your views now?

C.   Of course I haven't. Why should I?

P.   Because you must know there's an after-life now.

C.   I don't know anything of the kind, and don't believe any of the people who tell me all that nonsense. Who is this young lad, by the way, and why does he have to repeat to you everything I say?

P.   Because he can see and hear you, and I can't.

C.   Have you gone blind and deaf?

P.   Of course not. But you are now a spirit, and I

can't see spirits.

C. I am not a spirit. I don't believe in spirits and never have.

P. But surely you can't think you are still on this earth? Can't you remember what happened?

C. I remember feeling infernally ill. Then I lost consciousness, and after that I woke up feeling better than ever.

P. Yes, and then what happened?

C. Look here, Patmore, I resent all this interrogation and your writing down everything I say like a policeman.

P. Sorry, my dear Cliff, but I'm very much interested. You don't appear to realise that you are what we down here call dead, though I appreciate the fact that you feel very much more alive.

C. There's no down here about it. You talk as if I were standing on a cloud and you were below. I never heard such rubbish. The only thing that's the matter with me is that sometimes my sight and my hearing seem a bit queer.

P. You mean perhaps that we look a bit dim to you and sound rather far off?

C. Yes, in a sense.

P. That's because you are a spirit and we have still got physical bodies.

C. I refuse to believe that I am a spirit. There are no spirits. When we die that is the end of us. You annoy me. You always did annoy me when we got talking on this subject, because you will not face facts. You can't get round science, and science declares that we have evolved from monkeys. I'm going. I've had enough of this futile argument. We shall never convince one another, so what's the good of talking? Good-bye.

"When he'd cleared out, Mr. Patmore pulled a funny face and said he hadn't changed a bit and always went on like that when he was alive."

Other cases of people not being aware that they had died are described later in this book. On October 19th Grandpa came, this time to encourage those on earth to pray for others who had died. By this time Mrs. Patmore had come to share her husband's interest in the communications, but neither of them said anything about the latter to the boy's parents.

"During biscuits this morning we had occasion to think of grandpa, and lo, he turned up on a sudden and imparted a few things. We had just been having history about the protestants breaking off from the cathlics and the cathlics saying mass for the dead and all that, and we were wondering what grandpa and the spirits thought about it.

"Then all at once I saw old grandpa, and he said the protestants did quite wrong not to pray for people when they are what we call dead, because unselfish prayers are beautiful thoughts and make a lovely light round the spirits and help them a lot and let them know we are thinking of them too, which gives them pleasure and reminds them they are not forgotten.

"Grandpa said it is the parsons' fault that so many people don't pray for the spirits, because a lot of them make out that when we die we go to sleep till the day of resurrection, which grandpa says is all stuff and nonsense. He said when he was on earth he felt far more dead than alive, but now that he is supposed to be dead, he feels far more alive than dead. I've just been thinking that if mater knew about our intervues with grandpa and all he tells us, she'd think he was the devil dressed up in grandpa's clothing and come to tempt us. It does seem silly. If only the mater could open herself like Mr. and Mrs. P. to things it would be so much nicer, it would really."

The diary continued for another year, and in its entirety it fills two hundred pages. It is by no means concerned only with psychic communication, and provides a fascinating glimpse of life in a late Victorian fairly affluent household, seen through the eyes of a small boy. I have quoted only a small part of the psychic experiences of this boy, particularly those which he had before he came under the influence of his tutor, after the latter, through the child's clairvoyance, became interested in Spiritualism.

The diarist, from what we know of his later life, was as an adult more of a Theosophist than a Spiritualist. My purpose in giving the above extracts from the diary is to show how a boy, before he came under any adult influence, received psychically information about life after death which is in close accord with information from many other psychic sources. If the origin of his psychic experiences was not what it purports to be, what is the explanation of these experiences? This is a difficult question to answer. There are some who would agree with Mamma in her suspicions of the devil in respect of any supposed communications from beyond this life, and some psychical researchers might suggest that telepathy from some earthly mind could provide the explanation. All that can be said with certainty is that there are people who find such evidence convincing, while there are others who do not.

I ought to mention that communications similar to those described in the diary have been reported as having been received by other young children; but, so far as I know, none of them had the literary bent of the Boy Who Saw True.

TWO

Church Teaching
and Psychical Study

It was a demonstration of hypnosis which first aroused my curiosity about certain amazing capacities of the mind of which I had been entirely unaware. I began reading books on hypnosis, and this led me on to books about psychical phenomena, some of which have a connection with hypnotism.

Both my wife and I became fascinated by the subject, and together we read literally scores of books about psychic matters, mostly borrowed from Rugby Library. We were almost completely uncritical in our approach to psychical study. We knew nobody to advise us in the choice of books, and we just read anything we could get hold of. There were none written by those engaged in serious research. Most of them were concerned with mediumistic communications, allegedly from those who had died.

My interest was partly professional. During parish life I had come to the opinion that a considerable proportion of churchpeople had no real belief in the final statements of the Apostles' and the Nicene Creeds, the two creeds which are regularly used in the Anglican Church. The former ends with these words:— "... the resurrection of the body, and the life everlasting." The latter has as its final sentence:— "I look for the resurrection of the dead and the life of the world to come."

The creeds, of course, reflect the teaching of Jesus as it is found in the New Testament. About nothing are His statements more definite than about the continuance of life after death, a demonstration of which was provided by His resurrection.

My feeling that this Christian teaching was received with scepticism by many of those who called themselves Christians was supported by public opinion polls on the subject. Only about fifty per cent of 'active churchpeople', one of them reported, had any conviction that they would experience life of any kind after they had died.

This was largely because of the findings of science during the past century or so. Darwin, without meaning to, had dealt a devastating blow to religion. And later scientists came to feel that they had to define the universe in a completely materialistic way. The picture which they drew left no room for God and a life lived after death. Most people, in spite of this, still retain a vague kind of belief in a Deity, and call upon Him instinctively in time of crisis. Churchpeople continue to pray to Him regularly—but even to imagine the possibility of a life beyond death is another matter.

The Church of England prayer book is of little help in this direction. The fourth of the Thirty-Nine Articles at the end of the book is as follows:— "Christ did truly rise again from death, and took again His body, with flesh, bones, and all things appertaining to the perfection of man's nature; wherewith He ascended into heaven, and there sitteth, until He return to judge all men at the last day." The Athanasian Creed, the third of the Anglican Church creeds, says:— "All men must rise again with their bodies."

So it appears that the Church believes that not only does Christ live in heaven with a completely physical body but that that is what we shall do too—should our previous earthly life be of sufficient virtue. To any thinking person this is inconceivable. There were no such difficulties in the days when the Prayer Book was written, but the thoughts of the twentieth century are very different from those of the medieval world.

I think the Church is greatly to blame for allowing the conception of a material heaven peopled by physical human bodies to remain—or appear to remain—as part of its theology. I cannot imagine any of its hierarchy believing such nonsense.

I certainly had never thought of a future life of this nature, although I had never doubted that life after death was a reality. Now I was reading books which described at least the first stage of life after death and, more than that, the descriptions were given by those who were living that life—or so these books claimed.

The channels which were used for conveying this information were mediums, although many of them would have disowned the name—and certainly they were unlike the popular image of a medium. They were not making a living out of their psychic gifts; not that there is necessarily anything wrong in this. They were people to whom there came unbidden the information which they believed emanated from 'the other world', and who converted this information into the printed word. None of these books ever became best-sellers. They were not to be found in bookshops, except those which dealt in psychic literature. The great majority of people had never heard of them, so it is most unlikely that their authors made much financial gain from them.

Neither my wife nor I read these books with the idea of trying to find proof of the survival of death. We read them because much of what they contained had the ring of truth about it. It fitted in with what we believed about religion; it contradicted nothing of what was our understanding of the New Testament. On the contrary, it illuminated a great deal of Christian teaching, and made a reality of what had previously been a rather nebulous concept.

Why is the Bible the most widely read book in so much of the world? It is not simply because the Church declares that it is divinely inspired, but because there is something about it, and particularly about the Gospels, that appeals to the heart and mind as authentic; conforming to what the human spirit feels is true about life.

I would not compare the books which we were reading with the Bible, but they made something of the same kind of impact on us. I have come to know since that time that a great deal of rubbish has been published on the subject of life after death, and we were fortunate in reading those of greater quality—thanks, I suppose, to the judgement of the library committee which chose the books for their shelves.

The Church, generally, frowns upon psychical study, and there is reason for its disapproval. So much psychical material is written and published which is not only not worth reading but only too easily can mislead the gullible reader and result in most unfortunate effects upon his life.

On the other hand, it must not be forgotten that, on occasion, the reading of the Bible has been followed by the founding of strange sects which have had the most damaging effects upon their members.

Psychical study is not without its dangers. It needs guidance from those who are well versed in the subject—as indeed does study of the Bible. But I think that the Church is too severe in its widespread condemnation of the subject. Where there is the possibility of evil, the opposite is equally true.

The Church seems very negative in its consideration of matters of a transcendent nature. There is a great deal that is mystifying in life. When something evil, which is not easily explicable, appears in the behaviour of someone, the Church is prone to ascribe this to the influence of Satan or evil spirits.

When someone's life is suddenly and obviously changed for the better, God may rightly be thought to be behind the change, but the possible influence of angels or good spirits—'God's heavenly civil service', as my friend Canon John Pearce-Higgins would sometimes call them—is never mentioned.

Unseen evil powers are often inveighed against by the clergy, yet their counterparts who are on the side of God, so to speak, are ignored. I find this attitude reflected in the attitude of a good many churches towards life and religion generally. Human sinfulness is dwelt upon at great length, and it would certainly be foolish to ignore it as modern psychology is inclined to do. But human goodness and compassion are less emphasised by the churches.

To most non-Christians the crucifixion of Jesus must seem the central fact of the Christian faith, with the Cross as its symbol. The early Christians, but not some of the later ones, I think, had a better idea of what religion is about. They had neither empty crosses nor crucifixes with a suffering or dead Christ. The first crosses showed a living and victorious Jesus, arrayed in royal robes, which symbolised His conquest of sin and of death.

Too many Christians regard life negatively, as dominated by evil, whether on earth or in the ethereal regions, and it is true that Jesus taught that the earthly human experience is no bed of roses. But above all He was positive in His conviction that a good God was dominant, in spite of all appearances, whether in this world or beyond.

There is no basic reason why what is learnt through psychic channels should be ascribed to an evil source rather than a good one. It is unwise to assert that it must always come from either one or the other. But uncertainty should not preclude careful investigation of the phenomena, strange though they may often be.

It is partly because so much in psychical study is strange, and not at all understood by science, that a good many clergy ascribe its phenomena to diabolic origin. To them, anything essentially odd is suspect, as the likely work of the devil. Even if somebody is healed of some bodily infirmity that doctors have diagnosed as incurable, if the cure is not labelled as 'divine healing', blessed by the authority of the Church, they feel that it may well be Satan who is responsible.

People such as these help to give psychical research the bad name which sometimes it undeservedly has. There are other people who think that it is wrong to engage in psychical research because God does not intend that we should supplement our faith with a modicum of knowledge. I find this idea illogical.

Those very first Christians who built the Church were men and women of remarkable faith, and they emphasised the importance of this virtue. But their faith did not come from reading the New Testament, which had not yet been written, nor essentially from what are usually called 'religious experiences'.

Their faith was based upon what they were convinced was evidence of the most solid kind. Some of them had shared the earthly life of Jesus, and others had seen the miracles which He had performed. They had seen Him and talked with Him after His resurrection. They had no difficulty at all in believing in the new faith. Without these first-hand witnesses the Christian religion would not have begun.

Why should it be thought that God wants to make it all so much more difficult for us today, in the cold, scientific society in which we live? Can God grudge us knowledge to help to strengthen our faith in this materialistic age? It would seem to be most unlikely.

Nevertheless, as I have said, information that is received psychically must be scrutinised as thoroughly as is practicable, to determine whether alternative explanations are possible or probable.

More than ten years ago I wrote a booklet which was an introduction to psychical study. My bishop, the Bishop of Coventry, who at that time was Cuthbert Bardsley, wrote a foreword to it. In this is the following :—

> "The subject is one that has been lamentably neglected by the Church, with the result that foolish and unwise people have tended to give it unwholesome and unnatural twists. Thus many sane people have been prevented from exercising their minds in the field of psychical research.
>
> "I hope that this booklet will do something to restore the balance, and show that the psychical experience of our present age can be, as Mr. Barham says, 'a kind of new revelation from God to combat and overcome the materialism of today.' "

Before I met Dr. Bardsley when he became Bishop of Coventry in 1956, he had had an interest in psychical research for many years. I kept the bishop up to date, as far as possible, with contemporary cases of special significance, and would lend him books which I thought were of particular value. His favourite general book on the subject was *The*

Imprisoned Splendour, by Raynor C. Johnson, a scientist who was Master of Queen's College, University of Melbourne (Hodder & Stoughton 1953). This is an excellent book, and still well worth reading although it is somewhat outdated by research done since the time of its writing.

The bishop's favourite book concerned chiefly with evidence for the survival of death was *Beyond the Horizon* by Grace Rosher (James Clarke & Co. Ltd. 1961). I lent the bishop this book soon after it was published, and he gave it to some of his friends to read, as he was particularly impressed by it.

One of these borrowers was a very old admiral, almost all of whose relations and friends had died. After he had read the book, he became completely convinced of the desirability of entering the life which follows this. The bishop told me that he would rather embarrass him when they were talking together in their club, by saying in a very loud voice, as people who are as deaf as he was are apt to do, how greatly he wanted to die, to join those who were dear to him.

It was some time after this that there was arranged a conference, of which my bishop was the chairman. Most surprisingly it was organised by the Community of the Resurrection, a very influential body of the Anglican Church. It was surprising because the conference was concerned with various psychic subjects, including non-medical healing and mediumship of different kinds. On the last day, the final talk of the conference was to have been given by Grace Rosher, but she was ill and I, as a friend of hers who had made a study of the case, was asked to take her place.

I told her story, and answered questions as best I could. A little later a Scottish bishop came up to me and told me privately that this was the evidence that he had been waiting for—evidence not for his own benefit, but for the benefit of those in his diocese who were uncertain and anxious about the nature of post-mortem existence.

I will say something here about the unusual experience of Miss Rosher, but I will not go into detail, as I have described the case in my book, *Strange to Relate* (New Horizon 1980). Grace Rosher believed that her fiancé, Gordon Burdick, who had died in 1956, had, the following year, begun to communicate with her through what is popularly known as 'automatic writing'. This writing described the kind of life which he had been living since his death, and the general conditions which obtained in his new world. There was nothing particularly new, I think, in these communications. Very similar accounts of the life after this can be found in many books. What was different about Miss Rosher's experience, compared with that of nearly all of the other writers, was that her case provided confirmatory evidence which some researchers found to be of a convincing nature.

THREE

Grace Rosher and Gordon Burdick

The gist of this evidence was that Miss Rosher's communications, allegedly from Gordon Burdick, were not in Grace Rosher's handwriting but in one that was significantly comparable with Gordon's writing before he died. There was not just a general similarity, but a most extraordinary correspondence, for which one of the country's leading handwriting experts could find no orthodox explanation. Critics, of course, suggested that Miss Rosher was reproducing subconsciously handwriting with which she was extremely familiar. But the expert, after a painstaking and indeed microscopic examination of what had been written, said that this was quite impossible, however likely it might seem to those with little or no knowledge of graphology.

Later in this case I was involved in another investigation by the graphologist in which a similar phenomenon had taken place, but with a difference. This time the communicator was completely unknown to Grace Rosher, which rather confounds the previous critics.

It would not be fitting in a book of this kind to enter into a lengthy exposition of the possible nature of a future life, using the evidence of psychical research. As I have said, there are a great number of books which have been written about this, and the better ones—although of course this is a subjective judgement on my part—are in substantial agreement.

Those which enter into great detail, giving an almost hour by hour description, I find unconvincing. Whatever may be the kind of existence we could experience after this life, it is bound to be different in so many ways that, in my opinion, only generalities can filter through to us earth-bound mortals.

We have some idea of what the moon looks like, and to a much lesser extent we know something about the appearance of some of the planets. We have seen television pictures of them and, in the case of the moon and of Mars, they seem not unearthlike and so not difficult to comprehend. Even the more nebulous television pictures of some planets other than Mars are comprehensible in as far as what they show is material; that is to say, composed of substances with which we are familiar on earth.

But when I think about the nature of life after death, I often remind myself of a comment which M. Piccard made after his descent in a bathysphere in 1959 to a depth of the sea far beyond what had previously been achieved. He told an interviewer that what he had seen was so unlike anything formerly beheld by a human being that any detailed description was impossible. He had had a most wonderful experience, but one that was literally indescribable.

How unlikely must it be, therefore, that anyone who has left this terrestrial life can be precise in what he tells us of his new existence. The most that can be looked for, I think, is some understanding of the general principles that govern the life after this — always provided, of course, that the communications are what they purport to be.

In what follows in this chapter, and in the succeeding ones, where mediumistic communications are concerned, for the sake of brevity there will be a minimal use of such terms as 'purported', 'alleged' and 'claimed'.

Sometimes it may appear that I am completely convinced about the truth of some psychically received information, but whatever may be the value of any communication which may come from another sphere of life, I would emphasize that there is no possible scientifically acceptable manner in which its unearthly origin can be proved.

It might be of interest to add that present-day scientists are not nearly so fond of using the word, 'proof', as the general public suppose. They are rightly much more cautious than the scientists of earlier centuries. These scientists were often confident that they had said the last word on their particular subject. Now it is realised that the more that is discovered the more there is to be learned, and that even what seemed to be fundamental truth can occasionally be found to be false.

Something else I would add is that however real and honest a communicator may be, and however gifted a medium may prove, there may be a contribution from the unconscious mind of the latter which could distort the communication. This is where the comparison of various communications from different mediums can be useful, although it should be borne in mind that a general 'psychic picture' of the next world is possessed by most mediums through what they have been told or read.

Miss Rosher, as it happened, had very little knowledge of psychic matters. She was a devout Anglican, with quite conventional religious views. What she had read casually in newspapers or magazines about psychic phenomena she had found distasteful, if not repellent.

When the writing so like that of Gordon Burdick appeared—quite spontaneously, as Grace had no intention of trying to produce the phenomena—she was rather suspicious regarding its origin. She had read some psychology, and was aware that her unconscious mind might be responsible for what was happening. She resolved that if the graphologist's report supported this explanation she would put a stop to the writing; but as his findings ruled out the theory she continued, and finally her book was published and aroused a great deal of interest.

I remember seeing her in a television interview. She was put into one corner of the studio, and instructed to try to obtain a communication from Gordon while someone else was being interviewed. I need hardly say that no writing appeared. The ignorance of the media of the conditions in which psychic phenomena are likely to appear is quite remarkable, but of course this ignorance is widespread.

It was soon after this that I went to see a bishop (not my own Bishop of Coventry) about an article he wanted me to write for *The Church Times* on psychical research. Unfortunately at that time the paper would not consider an article on such a dubious subject, so it was never published. During our conversation the bishop mentioned that a few days earlier Grace Rosher had come to see him, at his request. Like the B.B.C. interviewer, the bishop without any warning asked her to produce Gordon's handwriting while he watched. Again nothing happened. I explained to the bishop that this was not the way to go about it, and suggested that he saw Grace again, but this time made in advance an appointment, so to speak, with Gordon. My suggestion was followed and the writing, which so interested the bishop, appeared.

Here is some of the information which was received from Gordon, and which could be paralleled by similar accounts from other comparable sources :—

When a person who has lived a reasonably 'good' life dies, upon regaining consciousness he is met by those dear to him or her who have died earlier. There are exceptions to this, as I mention later on in this book.

The new surroundings which are experienced are so earth-like in appearance, and the body of the one who has just died, and the bodies of the others, seem so like they were before death, that sometimes there is difficulty in realising that death has, indeed, taken place. This is more often the case when the death has been sudden and unexpected. When there is a full realisation of the truth of the matter, life very similar to that on earth is lived, although this worldly aspect of the new life is only temporary. This earth-like life will be succeeded sooner or later—the time being determined by spiritual progress—by, as it were, a second death, which is really an awakening to a higher state of consciousness, where earthly appearances are unnecessary, and further spiritual progress can be made. Gordon deals with this subject as follows :—

"You know there are many different spheres in this world, many of them far higher than the one I and those of my family and yours are now living on. These spheres are all much more beautiful than even this one and those who live there are all more highly evolved spiritually than we who have only recently come to this world.

"Very few of those I have met have ever entered these higher spheres and then only for a short visit. The atmosphere is so rarified and the light so brilliant that one could not endure it for long. One must have become more used to life on this spiritual plane of thought and grown in spirituality before one can proceed to the next and higher plane . . . . I don't know how long it takes to qualify for entry into one of these higher spheres, but probably hundreds of years of earthly time. I am at present very satisfied with this one and in no hurry to move up higher which, no doubt, shows I am very far from being ready to do so!

"To return once again to the Heavenly spheres, although we cannot enter them until we are ready, those higher Beings who live there can visit the lower ones like ours, and those that are lower still. When they come to the planes below them it is to help and teach. They are nearer the angels who are the messengers of God. There really are angels and they are Beings not just thoughts, but Beings of a higher order than ourselves, that is, than ordinary human beings."

After all the more advanced states of consciousness have been experienced, finally there is union with God.

It is only from the first stage of the after-life that communications which may seem convincing come. As I have suggested above, even in these cases there are probably only approximate descriptions. The later stages of consciousness appear to be almost completely indescribable, although occasionally attempts have been made.

Grace Rosher was told that, after death, life was by no means boring. "This is not a dull place," Gordon wrote. "Life is full of interest and activity. Then one can study, there is so much to learn, one can take up the study of subjects one wanted to study on Earth and never had time to. When you come here you can carry on with your singing and painting and anything else you want to do."

Religion, although not of a formal type, plays a very prominent part :—

"We pass from an ever-changing world where nothing is permanent into an unchanging world where at last we find permanence and stability. We see life stretching out before us endlessly in a universe full of wondrous possibilities and opportunities. We come into a world where God is fully realised as a very living Presence, unseen but very near, and one is caught up with a wonderful understanding of the infinite love of God that embraces all creation, and so are lost in wonder, love and praise when we realise that this is life as it was meant to be for all to inherit.

"Yet those who have wasted or degraded their lives on earth cannot enter this happy life at first, not until they have learnt their lessons and redeemed the past. We all have to work out our own salvation sooner or later in one world or the other, and no other can do it for us."

This is a reminder that by no means everyone, when they die, enter into a life of happiness.

"If a man or woman have lived very selfish lives and never cared for anyone but themselves, they find themselves—often to their great surprise—in very squalid surroundings and with people of the same kind. They are usually very disgusted, and it has to be explained to them that it is their own doing. 'As a man soweth, so shall he reap.' These people are told that they can improve their lot if they want to, but they must start just where they are by learning to be good neighbours.

"Afterwards they can go and give help to those whose lot in life has been made harder by their greed and selfishness. When they see—as they can—the harm or suffering they have caused they are often very sorry and ashamed and want to make amends. That is the beginning of spiritual progress."

But not all of those who have lived lives which seem to be spiritually bankrupt have to undergo a period of suffering.

"There are others who have lived hard and cruel lives, because they have never known any better; they have known nothing of God as a loving Father. They are quite ignorant as to spiritual truths. Life to them has been merely a struggle for existence and they are little better than animals in their way of living. They are often the victims of 'Man's inhumanity to man'. These poor souls need love more than most and it is marvellous to see how they respond to the tenderness shown to them. They do not want to go back to their old ways. Life is a revelation to them, a wonderland they had no conception of. I sometimes have these people to deal with and they are the easiest to help and teach. Love is something they have never had shown to them. You would marvel at the different types of humanity pouring over here continually, each one dealt with separately according to his or her special need."

I will end this thumbnail sketch of our possible future existence with Gordon's answer to Grace's question, "Is your world a world of illusion?"

"I can only say that the world of illusion is created by thinking in terms of the finite and material. Spirit is not an illusion, it is true and real, so when we come to think in terms of the spiritual nature of life and the whole Universe, we are no longer living in a world of illusion or unreality. I think that in our earthly life we are often living in an illusory world because the transient nature of life itself is an illusion and we place too much importance on the things which seem real, but are not. I find that in this real world we have a feeling of permanence and the fear of loss is no longer in our consciousness."

I have found nothing in the communications which Miss Rosher received which is contrary to the ethical teachings of Jesus. On the contrary, they emphasize them and help us to understand their implications. There are certain theological points which Gordon makes that might be thought by some to be unorthodox, although I have not heard of criticism in this respect. It is particularly significant, I think, that several members of the Community of the Resurrection, a body of considerable theological erudition, were extremely impressed by the book which Miss Rosher wrote, and invited her more than once to come to talk to them.

I don't know whether they questioned the theology of the communications. They told me of no such doubts when I met some of them. It may be, of course, that Gordon was not far advanced in theological knowledge—indeed he admitted as much. As Canon Pearce-Higgins wrote in his introduction to the book, "the communications given in these [theological] matters would only serve to stress the importance of not attributing 'omniscience' to those who have comparatively recently passed over".

Before I finish this chapter, I ought to add a word of warning. Anyone who has made a study of psychic matters knows that there can be very real danger in deliberate experimentation in automatic writing, and also in that which is commonly called 'inspired'. I have personal and unhappy experience of this; not that I attempted anything in that direction myself, but a friend of mine unfortunately did.

He was a vicar whom I knew well, and of whom Janet and I were particularly fond. His sister found that she was able to produce automatic writing, and continued to do so 'for fun'. Unwisely he decided to try to do the same. In a sense he was extremely successful. He watched his hand write, without any conscious effort on his part, messages which, they declared, were from exalted spirits close to God. He believed this, and soon found himself writing, in this way, grossly abusive letters, which the spirits insisted he should send to certain eminent people, including among them his bishop.

My wife and I, to whom he confided all this, realised that the spirits in question were either evil entities from another realm of being, or, much more probably, productions of our friend's unconscious mind. Tactfully we tried to convince him of this; whereupon we immediately received a rather impolite message ourselves! The scurrilous letters were sent, with the result that the career of a priest greatly loved by his parishioners was ended. Some time later he realised his mistake, but by then the damage had been done.

FOUR

The Majority Report

In 1937, Cosmo Lang, the Archbishop of Canterbury, appointed a committee to investigate Spiritualism, the growth of which was a cause for concern in the Anglican Church. After two years this committee published both a majority and a minority report.

These reports were presented to the bishops of the Church of England, but the rest of the clergy and the laity had no opportunity to read the reports, as their publication was forbidden.

It was understood that the findings of the majority report were so confusing that no clear guidance was given to Christian people. However, when I asked one of the signatories of the majority report, Dr. Matthews, the Dean of St. Paul's, why he thought the report had been suppressed, he told me it was because it would have shocked churchpeople too much.

Whatever was the true reason for the report's suppression, the censorship remained until 1979, when *The Christian Parapsychologist* received official permission to publish it. In 1947 it had been leaked to *Psychic News,* but the general public was not aware of it, and probably even now know little about it.

I first came across the report about twenty-five years ago, and since then I have often discussed it with friends who were interested in psychical research. A précis of it is given in my previous book. I think it is a valuable document, although it was produced so long ago. It raises many points which are still of considerable interest to those who are concerned about the attitude of the Anglican Church towards psychical phenomena in their relation to religion.

One thing that seems clear from the report is that some of those who signed it had very divergent views. At one end of the spectrum, as it were, there were conventional orthodox churchmen: at the other were those who were convinced that psychic phenomena provided convincing evidence for the survival of death and communication between ourselves and those 'on the other side'. The views which these two categories held might have seemed to have been mutually exclusive.

But one of the most remarkable things about this report was that those who were obviously deeply suspicious of anything to do with psychic phenomena should put their names to it, when it contained statements that seemed to favour Spiritualism. It was also surprising, perhaps, that those of the opposing standpoint should sign something that included statements which supported orthodox Anglican doctrine.

To illustrate the difference between the two points of view, I have abstracted from the report some of those sections which seem pro-Spiritualism, and others which appear opposed to Spiritualism. It will be noticed that the former sections do not contain the words, 'Spiritualism' or 'Spiritualist', as do the latter sections; and this may be significant.

An interpretation of this could be that those who seemed to be in favour of Spiritualism were not in favour of a separate body calling itself a religion, but rather were advocating that what truth there might be in the Spiritualist position should be introduced into the teaching of the Anglican Church; and indeed that is suggested at the end of the report.

This is the position in which I find myself. I could never become a Spiritualist, yet I believe that those psychic phenomena which are relevant to religion should be taken into account in the formulation of Christian theology.

Here are the two abstracts. First the pro-Spiritualist one. I have numbered the various sections for ease of reference.

1   It is clearly true that the recognition of the nearness of our friends who have died, and of their progress in the spiritual life, and of their continuing concern for us, cannot do otherwise, for those who have experienced it, than add a new immediacy and richness to their

belief in the Communion of Saints. There seems to be no reason at all why the Church should regard this vital and personal enrichment of one of her central doctrines with disfavour, so long as it does not distract Christians from their fundamental gladness that they may come, when they will, into the presence of their Lord and Master, Jesus Christ Himself, or weaken their sense that their fellowship is fellowship in Him.

2   The experiences which many people have found most convincing are of a kind which could hardly occur in the atmosphere of scientific investigation. They are sporadic, occasional and highly individual. They could not possibly be repeated, or submitted to statistical analysis. It is worth while to notice in this connection that in the ordinary affairs and beliefs of human life we do not ask for scientific verification of this kind. We accept many things as certain in the realm of personal relationships upon the basis of direct insight. When we say that we know our friends, we mean something very different from saying that we can give a scientific and verifiable account of them. But we are none the less sure of our knowledge. Similar certainties are to be found in the sphere of mystical experience. It may well be that in this matter of the evidence for the survival of the human personality after death, we are dependent upon exactly this same kind of insight, and that scientific verification, though valuable where it can be obtained, is of secondary importance, and only partially relevant.

3   Certain outstanding psychic experiences of individuals, including certain experiences with mediums, make a strong *prima facie* case for survival and for the possibility of spirit-communications, while philosophical, ethical and religious considerations may be held to weigh heavily on the same side. When every possible explanation of these communications has been given, and all doubtful evidence set aside, it

is very generally agreed that there remains some element as yet unexplained. We think that it is probable that the hypothesis that they proceed in some cases from discarnate spirits is the true one.

4 Those who have the assurance that they have been in touch with their departed friends may rightly accept the sense of enlargement and of unbroken fellowship which it brings.

5 There is no reason why we should not accept gladly the assurance that we are still in the closest contact with those who have been dear to us in this life, and who are going forward, as we seek to do ourselves, in the understanding and fulfilment of the purpose of God.

The second, anti-Spiritualist, abstract is as follows:—

1 We cannot ignore the fact that at least one considerable Spiritualist organisation is definitely anti-Christian in character.

2 Many alleged communications seem, indeed, to fall below the highest Christian standards of understanding and spiritual insight; and indeed below the level of spiritual insight and mental capacity shown by the communicators while still in this life. While there is insistence upon the supremacy of love comparable with the New Testament assertion that 'God is Love', the accounts sometimes given of the mediatorial work of Christ frequently fall very far below the full teaching of the Christian Gospel, seeming to depend rather upon some power of working a miracle of materialisation (in the Resurrection appearances) than upon a radical and final acceptance of the burden of guilt of man's sin, and a victory so wrought for us upon the Cross.

3 It has been seen, in the account of the evidence submitted to our Committee, that so far as rigid scientific tests are concerned very little, if anything, remains both verifiable and inexplicable out of the

whole mass of paranormal phenomena. Modern psychological knowledge has revealed a wide range of powers and of possible sources of misunderstanding in our subconscious or unconscious mind. When these are combined with the possibility of direct thought-transference, or telepathy, many of the communications delivered through mediums seem capable of explanation.

4　It is abundantly clear, as Spiritualists themselves admit, that an easy credulity in these matters opens the door to self-deception and to a very great amount of fraud. We were greatly impressed by the evidence of this which we received, and desire to place on record a most emphatic warning to those who might become interested in Spiritualism from motives of mere curiosity, or as a way of escaping from the responsibility of making their own decisions as Christians under the guidance of the Holy Spirit.

5　We cannot avoid the impression that a great deal of Spiritualism as organised has its centre in man rather than in God, and is, indeed, materialistic in character. To this extent it is a substitute for religion, and is not, in itself, religious at all. We were impressed by the unsatisfactory answers received from practising Spiritualists to such questions as 'Has your prayer life, your sense of God, been strengthened by your spiritualistic experiences?' This explains in great part the hesitation of many Christians to have anything to do with it.

6　It may stimulate curiosity in the bizarre. It may offer consolation upon terms which are too easy . . . . It is often held that the practice of Spiritualism is dangerous to the mental balance, as well as to the spiritual condition, of those who take part in it and it is clearly true that there are some cases where it has become obsessional in character . . . . The view has often been held, with some degree of Church authority, that psychic phenomena are real, but that they proceed from evil spirits.

There are some comments which I should like to make about certain of the statements contained in these abstracts. To take the first abstract:— it begins with an assertion that 'communication' is of great value for those who experience it, and supports the doctrine of the Communion of Saints.

There is a proviso, however, that such communication should not take the place of the relationship which Christians have with Jesus. And it is certainly true that there is a danger here. In the services of at least some Spiritualist churches the most important part is what is usually called the 'demonstration of clairvoyance', when a medium believes that he enables members of the congregation to communicate with those who have died.

The second section states that research of a scientific kind cannot expect to achieve the sort of results which are found in a more congenial atmosphere. The findings of psychical research since the writing of the majority report support this view. Experiences of a psychic or mystical nature can be as convincing as, or indeed more convincing than, the results of successful laboratory experiments. If this is denied, and scientific proof insisted upon, the point might be made that no scientific proof is available to validate the religious beliefs of Christian people.

The third section is very important. The case for survival and communication demonstrated by psychic means is strong, and is supported by philosophical, ethical and religious arguments. Then comes a most positive statement: 'We think that it is probable that the hypothesis that they [communications] proceed in some cases from discarnate spirits is the true one.'

It is remarkable that the anti-Spiritualist members of the committee should have felt able to accept this statement, and also the assertion that those who are convinced that they have been in communication with friends who have died need feel no guilt about it, but, on the contrary, should accept it gladly.

A summary of the first abstract might go something like this:— *The Committee feels that sometimes there is genuine communication between those on earth and those who have died. The evidence for this is strong, although proof of a scientific nature is unlikely to be obtained. Those who experience such communication should welcome it as something of great value, but should take care that it does not take precedence over the relationship which Christians have with Jesus.*

The second abstract presents a very different view of the problem. It begins with the statement that some Spiritualists are opposed to Christianity. Probably the great majority of Spiritualists are anti-Church, but not, I think, anti-Christian. What is true is that their interpretation of the New Testament differs in certain respects from orthodox doctrine, as reflected in the World Council of Churches.

An example of this is found in the second section, and concerns the meaning of the Atonement, which is often regarded by Spiritualists as a supreme example of love rather than 'a radical and final acceptance of the burden of guilt of man's sin'.

Section 3 stresses the unsatisfactory nature of psychic evidence from a scientific point of view. Since the majority report was written, the idea of telepathy has become more acceptable to scientific thought. Also there is growing evidence for the reality of psychokinesis—the manipulation of matter by mind. This tends to weaken the case for the intervention of discarnate beings to account for communication and for physical psychic phenomena.

The fourth section mentions credulity and fraud. Fraud, I think, is less common than is generally supposed, but credulity is widespread among Spiritualists and is, perhaps, the chief weakness of their position.

There is a warning against 'mere curiosity' as a reason for becoming interested in Spiritualism—but curiosity surely is a prime motive in enquiry into anything unknown. The advance of all knowledge is due to curiosity!

Christians are also warned against Spiritualism 'as a way of escaping from the responsibility of making their own decisions under the guidance of the Holy Spirit'. There is some sense in this, but on the other hand can Christians always be sure that they really are guided by the Holy Spirit? In a time of war the Christian hierarchy of opposing countries have often been certain that the Holy Spirit has guided their respective governments in a just conflict against wicked foes.

Section 5 charges Spiritualism with being materialistic, and a substitute for religion. I think this is at least partly true. Religion is concerned with spiritual values, and there is nothing spiritual, in that sense, in the survival of death and communication by those who survive, crucially important though these matters may be. Some Spiritualists are also members of more orthodox churches, and probably share with others of their denomination a religious outlook upon life. But there are many Spiritualists, I think, whose chief concern is with the continuation of life beyond death, and who are not really concerned with a relationship with God which is at the centre of all religion.

The last section makes claims some of which are difficult to substantiate. It is true that Spiritualism 'may stimulate curiosity in the bizarre'. But this is not a valid criticism. Those who are not Christians might say that much in Christianity is bizarre or fantastic. They would include under that heading the Incarnation and the Resurrection of Jesus.

I cannot understand the charge that Spiritualism 'may offer consolation upon terms that are too easy'. If communication with a relative or friend who has died is found consoling, what can be wrong with that? It has been said that it was the lack of consolation that bereaved people found in the Church after the First World War that accounted for the growth of Spiritualism at that time; and certainly the teaching of the Church about life after death is most inadequate.

Another criticism of Spiritualism is that it is a cause of insanity. There is no doubt that some Spiritualists become insane, but so do some members of more orthodox churches. So far as I know, comparative statistics are not available.

Finally, it is suggested that evil spirits are operative in psychic phenomena. This is impossible to disprove, but even so, surely the opposite is equally, if not more, probable. Why should not good spirits play a part in a universe governed by that good God in whom Christians believe?

It is difficult to summarise this second abstract. It seems that there are several charges against Spiritualism which are the result of prejudice rather than reason. Nevertheless there is also criticism which appears to be just. Science is an uncertain ally of Spiritualists. It cannot prove the truth of survival, and probably never will. Credulity is only too easy, and 'opens the door to self-deception'. Spiritualists are apt to concentrate their attention upon the future life, and neglect what is usually considered 'the religious life' here and now.

If this attitude which is displayed by the 'orthodox' members of the Committee is compared with that of the others, it will be seen that there is, at least, one point of agreement. Conclusive evidence of survival and communication is extremely unlikely. That view is not shared by most Spiritualists, who often claim to have 'cast-iron proof' of them.

Apart from this, can the opinions expressed in the two abstracts be combined to form an acceptable whole, as those who signed the report must have believed?

Against Spiritualism there are charges of fraud, of credulity, of causing insanity and of the involvement of evil spirits. Another danger is that Spiritualism tends to be man-centred rather than God-centred.

Nevertheless the case for survival and communication is strong, and is supported by philosophical, ethical and religious considerations. Communication with deceased relatives and friends, sometimes at least, is probably genuine and is to be welcomed by those who experience it, so long as it does not distract them from their relationship with Christ.

The final paragraph of the report presents the general conclusions of the Committee :—

If Spiritualism, with all aberrations set aside and with every care taken to present it humbly and accurately, contains a truth, it is important to see that truth not as a new religion, but only as filling up certain gaps in our knowledge, so that where we already walked by faith, we may now have some measure of sight as well.

It is in our opinion important that representatives of the Church should keep in touch with groups of intelligent persons who believe in Spiritualism. We must leave practical guidance in this matter to the Church itself.

There has obviously been a compromise between the divergent points of view. It is a cautious statement, and gives no support to Spiritualism considered as a religion, which most Spiritualists insist that it is. It does give encouragement to those who believe that psychical research and experience may prove of considerable importance for people who seek for religious truth.

It is greatly to be regretted that the Church has not followed the suggestion that it should keep in touch with the more intelligent Spiritualists, who do not exhibit the aberrations complained of, and who maintain a properly critical attitude towards the mysterious phenomena with which they are concerned.

FIVE

Can Mediumship be Convincing ?

Most people, I think, although they have never had a sitting with a medium, have some idea of what takes place. They know that the medium tells the sitter what she hears or sees in a paranormal manner, and that sometimes figures are described by her which correspond closely with the appearance of deceased relations or friends of the sitter as he remembers them.

Messages from 'the other side', relayed by the medium, can provide impressive evidence that a discarnate person is communicating, although it is always possible to provide alternative theories—however improbable they may seem.

Many of those who have long experience of mediumship are of the opinion that more convincing than the majority of the sittings of the above type of mediumship—usually termed 'mental mediumship'—are those which are provided by a Direct Voice medium. This is because, at these, the sitters themselves can hear voices which claim to be the voices of those who live in the life beyond the present one. This is not because they suddenly become psychically gifted, but because the voices are as audible as any other sound in this physical world.

No hallucination or hypnosis is involved, as it is perfectly simple to tape-record all that takes place. It has been suggested that the medium is a ventriloquist who projects his disguised voice so that it seems to the sitters that it comes, not from him, but from the thin air a little distance away.

But ventriloquism needs light to foster the illusion, and Direct Voice sittings are nearly always held in the dark. Of course, the possibility of fraud must always be considered, involving hidden accomplices and electronic aids. But ultimately everything must depend on the voice itself, what the voice says, and the manner in which the information is conveyed.

The process may be compared with a telephone conversation with a friend, say, in Australia. Could someone definitely recognise his friend as his voice comes through the telephone? I should like to quote three paragraphs from my book, *Strange to Relate,* which originally appeared in the booklet which I have mentioned. In reply to a similar question, I wrote:—

"I think you could, providing you knew him sufficiently well, and the conversation was of a reasonable length. The line might be bad, so that you could not hear some of his words. He might have a poor memory, and be unable to remember events you think he should. Transmitted in an artificial way, his voice might not sound exactly as you remembered it. And yet you would recognise very quickly, I think, his manner of speaking, and indeed his pattern of thought. Any doubt you might have would soon be removed by your recognition of the small personal idiosyncrasies that were his and nobody else's in the whole world.

"Of course there is little doubt that a competent actor, who was acquainted with all the mannerisms of your friend, and who had been provided with a suitable script, could deceive you for a minute or two. But as soon as you began a conversation the actor's pretence would surely fail. He would find himself scriptless, and unable to maintain the part, particularly if his mental calibre was conspicuously inferior to that of your friend.

"I have been present many times at a Leslie Flint sitting, when voices have spoken which have been recognised as the unmistakable expression of the personality of someone—a relation or friend—who had died. Now it seems to me that if there are large numbers of people who say they definitely recognise their friends and relatives who have died, when they communicate in this way, by their distinctive manner of speaking and habit of thought, apart from personal facts which may be given, in much the same way that they might be recognised in a telephone conversation, then it is as good evidence that communication is indeed taking place as you can hope to get."

What really happens at a Direct Voice sitting? Suppose that someone who has died could speak in this way, what mechanism might be involved? The theory advanced by the mediums themselves invokes the use of the mysterious substance known as *ectoplasm*. This, it is said, is a volatile material which exists in different degrees of density.

Usually it is invisible to the eye, although, it is claimed, sometimes capable of being seen or photographed in infra-red light. The only occasion when it is visible in ordinary light—generally very dim—is at a materialisation séance, when it is employed to 'build up' the materialised figure.

It is thought that ordinary light inhibits the production of ectoplasm, which is the reason why Direct Voice sittings are held in the dark. I do not feel that this is the true explanation, as occasionally the phenomenon occurs in normal lighting. It is more probable that the requirement of darkness is a psychological necessity on the part of the medium. I am sure the sceptic will suggest that the medium uses the darkness as a cover for fraud. I have already mentioned this possibility, and undoubtedly fraud has sometimes taken place. But one rotten apple in a barrel—or even a few—does not prove that all the apples are bad.

I have a description of what it is alleged happens behind the scenes, as it were, at a Direct Voice sitting. I tape-recorded it during a visit to Leslie Flint, who is probably the best known Direct Voice medium alive at this time. I had taken a small group to this sitting, and one of them asked a question of a voice which came out of the darkness.

The voice was that of Mickey, who has been closely associated with Leslie Flint for many years, and who says that as a teenager he was killed in a traffic accident two or three generations ago. He acts as a helper on 'the other side', he says; and his task is to assist those who find it difficult to speak, and to relay their communications if necessary. The questioner asked Mickey if he could explain how the voices were produced. Here is part of the tape-recorded answer:—

"What one must bear in mind is that all methods of communication, whether it is in this form or any other, is basically a mental thing. And therefore, when a person comes to speak to you—when the scientist whose job it is to build up the voice-box from the ectoplasm supplied by the medium [has finished his work]: when it is all arranged and built up ready for the communicator, the transmission of their thought into sound, via the voice-box, is quite an art in itself. One has to learn how to manipulate it, and you've got to concentrate the mentality on saying certain things—invariably things that really are evidential to the recipient.

"And what one has to bear in mind most of all is that all communication is artificial—it must be. You see, the majority of people who go to a séance—to this kind of séance, that is—they say 'If that voice speaks to me in so-and-so's voice I'll believe it.' And the point is that it doesn't always sound like the identical voice, because what produces the actual voice is, and must be, artificial. It cannot be under any circumstances the identical voice, because they are not using the same physical body or the same vocal organs under the same conditions.

"What is actually happening is that they are trying to convert their thoughts into sound via the voice-box; the voice-box being artificial; temporarily constructed from ectoplasm, and kept in being, as far as possible, by the scientist who produces it and utilises it. And I don't see how you can get the identical voice, the identical tone. Occasionally the voice *is* reproduced; another time it takes a long time to get anything like the original voice. "

In this communication we are asked to imagine a discarnate scientist constructing, from ectoplasm obtained from the medium, a 'voice-box' which acts as a kind of transformer to convert the communicator's thoughts into words which are audible in the normal way to the sitters at a séance. If this seems incredible, perhaps it would be fair to point out that life without a physical body seems equally incredible, and yet millions of religiously-minded people throughout the world are convinced of the truth of this.

In any case, as I have said, in Direct Voice mediumship the vital thing is the voice itself. From an evidential point of view it does not matter how the voice is produced. Mickey's statement is useful, however, in reminding us that the voice must be of an artificial nature, and cannot be expected to be a facsimile of the particular communicator's voice before death. Occasionally the resemblance may be striking, but it is not to be expected.

I ought to mention that on more than one occasion when Leslie Flint was tested—not in his own home—it was established that the voices did not come from his vocal organs.

One thing to be guarded against is wishful thinking. Some sitters may long to communicate with someone close to them who has died, and could read into a voice something that is not there.

So, from the point of view of psychical research, it is desirable to examine the recording of a voice which, it is alleged, emanates from a personality whose voice and manner of expression had become very widely known before his death, through radio or television. As I have indicated above, it is not simply the voice that is of great importance; it is the way in which thoughts are expressed and various idiosyncrasies revealed that are of particular significance.

I have in my possession a tape which meets these requirements, a tape which, it is claimed, records a half-hour's conversation between George Bernard Shaw six years after his death and two sitters at a private séance.

In 1956 with a few friends I had gone to have a sitting with Leslie Flint. After the sitting we chatted for a short time, and I remarked to Leslie that it seemed strange that while we were usually most intrigued with what took place, he rarely showed a comparable interest. He reminded us that he had been a Direct Voice medium for many years, giving several sittings every week, and so could not be expected to have the same reactions as his sitters.

But, he went on, something had happened a few weeks before which had especially impressed him. Often, when he had finished the day's sittings, he said, he would leave his ground-floor flat and go upstairs to have tea with a friend, an old lady who owned the house in which was the flat. On this occasion another friend was present, a young man; and as the three were talking Leslie had a feeling that someone else, unseen, wanted to join in. A tape recorder was switched on; the sitting began, and within a few moments G.B.S. made his entrance.

Apart from the eminence of the communicator, this séance was unusual in two respects. First, it was not held in complete darkness. The curtains were drawn, but a certain amount of light was coming through them. Secondly, Leslie went into trance and knew nothing of what happened until later, when he listened to the recording. Normally during a sitting he remained conscious and took part in the conversation.

I have no reason to doubt the *bona fides* of Mr. Flint, but when I obtained a copy of the tape recording it was of such interest that I felt I would like to know more of the circumstances in which it had been made. So I arranged a meeting with Mrs. Rose Creet, the owner of the house where the séance had taken place. Mrs. Creet believed implicitly in the phenomenon of Direct Voice. She could have been called gullible, but she was certainly a woman of integrity. She confirmed what Leslie had told us, and in particular she confirmed that the questions which she had asked G.B.S. were entirely spontaneous.

This meant that the suspicions of a sceptic that a dishonest medium had prepared a script to deceive an old lady were unwarranted, as much of what Shaw had to say consisted of responses to the questions and comments of Mrs. Creet; and the nature of the responses was such that it seemed impossible that they originated from the mind of Leslie.

Some friends who listened to the tape recording were considerably impressed by its Shavian flavour, although they had never heard Shaw speak. But the first really impressive evidence for the authenticity of Shaw's communication came from George Bishop, a former dramatic critic of the *Daily Telegraph,* who had been a friend of G.B.S. for a great many years. It was with some reluctance that he consented to listen to the tape; he had no faith in psychic phenomena of this nature. But as soon as he heard the voice on the tape his attention was rivetted, and he sat unmoving for the thirty minutes of the recording. When it was finished it was apparent that he was deeply moved, and he told me, "The mind and the mood are Shaw's."

The only difference that he had noticed, he said, between the voice of Shaw *post-mortem* and the Shaw whom he remembered was that the latter had a faster delivery than that on the tape. But he was in little doubt that it was Shaw himself who had spoken.

The value of this evidence was impaired by the fact that it was an old friend who was concerned, who might have been influenced by the mechanism of wish-fulfilment. So I was glad when I was asked to go to Broadcasting House to play the tape to some people who knew a good deal about Shaw, but had not been his friends. A B.B.C. talks producer, Jack Singleton, was in charge of the proceedings, and when he compared my tape with some recordings of Shaw made by the B.B.C. not long before he died, he was sufficiently impressed to suggest an experiment. He wanted to produce a radio programme in which a number of people who had known Shaw well would listen to the tape—about which they would have been told nothing in advance — and give their opinion about it. The programme was never made, so I can only assume that permission to produce it was not obtained.

Like George Bishop, the writer Laurence Easterbrook had known Shaw for many years, but was not, I think, a close friend. After he had heard the recording he wrote to me, "I found the G.B.S. recording interesting indeed. The more I think about it, the more impossible it seems for anyone but himself to have been responsible. It brought back to me the sense of infectious gaiety one got with him when he was in the family circle and not showing off. You felt the world with all its follies was tremendous fun, to be laughed at with gentleness and understanding."

Dame Sybil Thorndike did not agree about the 'not showing off'. She told me, "It sounds like Shaw putting on an act for people whom he despised intellectually."

J. B. Priestley did not believe that the voice was that of Shaw, but he admitted to me that George Bishop had known G.B.S. better than he had himself. In spite of Mr. Priestley's disbelief, he had the courtesy to listen to the whole of the tape without interruption.

Mae West had less patience. In Hollywood in 1974 I was taken to meet her by a friend of hers, and because of her interest in psychic matters I told her about the Shaw recording and started to play the tape. After ten minutes or so, she could bear it no longer. "Can't that old man talk!" she exclaimed impatiently. I took the hint, and stopped the tape recorder. The rest of the afternoon was spent most entertainingly, listening to Mae West telling us about her remarkable career and reading to us a chapter or two from the book she was writing.

I was in California for a lecture tour, the second I had made in the United States, and which concluded for me a decade during which I had done a great deal of speaking about psychical research.

Often during my talks I would mention the Shaw tape and play part of it. I never expressed an opinion as to its authenticity or otherwise. I have no qualification to do so.

I never met Shaw, and the only occasion when I heard his voice was during my visit to Broadcasting House. If I am asked, as I often am, whether I think the tape is genuine, in the sense that Shaw is communicating, I have to reply simply that I don't know.

Yet, without any encouragement on my part, the audiences which have heard the tape almost without exception expressed great interest in it, and in addition agreed that it was extremely Shavian in character. Some of the listeners who had often heard Shaw speak were particularly emphatic in supporting this view.

As I have just said, I don't know whether Shaw communicated through Leslie Flint or not. Nevertheless I have an opinion about it. First, as I have indicated, I do not believe that Mr. Flint has a mind which is capable of producing the spontaneous conversation that is heard on the tape. I refer here to his conscious mind, as I have learned to know it over the years. What the unconscious mind contains provides one of the largest question marks in the area of psychical research.

It is conceivable that some other mind in an earthly body, capable of Shavian expression, telepathically provided the material that emerged at the séance. It is also conceivable that a mischievous discarnate being personated Shaw deceased. Some people might even believe, I suppose, that the devil was responsible for what took place, in order to mislead the faithful and attract them to Spiritualism. All that can be done is to consider the evidence, and to decide, if you can, where the probability lies.

SIX

The Bernard Shaw Tape

Below is a transcript of the major part of the Shaw tape. This transcript, it goes without saying, is not nearly so impressive as the spoken word with its nuances of expression. There are a few preliminary comments I should like to make.

At the beginning of the conversation, "my good friend, Marshall" is mentioned. This is Dr. Charles Marshall, a regular communicator, who sometimes (we were told) helped others to communicate during sittings. He was a doctor who was particularly concerned with cancer research, and he died a generation or more ago. I heard from someone who knew his widow that she was convinced that he communicated with her through Leslie Flint, and helped her to continue his research.

G.B.S. says, "Can you hear me?" at the beginning of the recording. It is characteristic of Direct Voice séances that there may be gaps in the communication during which, it is claimed, the voices continue without being aware that they are unheard by the sitters.

"Finding a new way of putting over old joints" and "jigging it up with a bit of music" seem obvious allusions to the musical, *My Fair Lady*.

When Shaw is talking about friends whom he has met in his new life, "Henry", of course, is Sir Henry Irving, and "Oscar" is Oscar Wilde. "Bossey" (or "Boysie") was the nickname of a friend of Wilde.

The Wallerites were followers of the popular singer Waller. Some of them wore a badge with 'KOW' upon it—'Keen on Waller' — and were known as the Kows. I hope the above comments will be helpful.

As soon as Leslie Flint switched on the tape recorder, the séance began. He went into deep trance, and the two sitters heard a voice of whose identity they were unaware. The great majority of their questions or observations were from Mrs. Creet. [These are printed in normal type and the disembodied voice is printed in italics.]

Good evening.
Good evening.
Can you hear?
Yes, thank you.
Good. I must ask you to bear with me for a moment or two. It's a very long time since I was able to inhabit a body and speak in this way. One becomes a little unfamiliar with the body.
We are very glad to hear you.
Thank you very much. And I am certainly most glad to be here, and to be able to talk to you for a minute or two. My good friend Marshall has very kindly allowed me to come. Can you hear me?
Yes, thank you. We can hear you very well.
Good. I suppose the usual procedure is to introduce oneself since one is unseen by the recipients of the message.
Yes. We should very much like to know.
Well, my name probably will not convey very much to you. You may have casually heard it mentioned in conversation; or it may be possible that you were one of the very disappointed people who came out of the theatre grumbling about wasted money, after having seen one—or more perhaps if you ever went a second time, that is, to one of my plays. This is G.B.S.
Oh yes! I don't think we've been disappointed . . .
Well, perhaps you have found the play, or plays, should you have seen more than one, interesting enough. But nevertheless one becomes more and more conscious of the fact when you've been here for any length of time, such as I have, that no matter how much one's work may have meant when on earth, even to the ones who were fortunate enough, like myself, to make a little money out of them; nevertheless you cannot but help feel that they were very

puerile and very poor in comparison to that which one can achieve, and has achieved, over here. Nevertheless I am very grateful indeed for many of the compensations of the earthly existence; but I have no desire whatever to return, should it be possible, that is; to return to live it all over again, and become, as I believe some people say one does, someone else. The fact of having been George Bernard Shaw is enough for any one person for any time.

Oh, your name will last everlastingly I should think.

What a dreadful thought that is. Anyway I'm glad that my work at least is making work for others, and that they are still finding a new way of putting over old joints.

You were a wonderful old man, you know. You lived to a very great age.

I don't mind 'wonderful'; I rather object to the 'old'. Age is merely a matter of comparison.

Yes, that's quite true. You didn't believe in this, did you, when you were on the earth? How do you find it over there?

Well, I must admit it was a very great surprise. I think the surprise of finding that I was still alive, and yet I was dead, was in itself a very great disappointment to me.

Why? You just wanted to finish, did you?

Well, I could see no point in continuing. After all's said and done, I could see no point in a life after death. I think that an earthly existence such as I experienced was enough for any one man; and if God was a God of love, He surely wouldn't permit another continuation of that. However, I've changed a little since then.

Yes; well, the continuation is very much more pleasant than it has been on the earth, isn't it?

You seem to know more about it than I do! May I be allowed to say, madam, since you have not yet arrived here, by what right can you tell me that it's better over here?

Well, as a matter of fact I've been well-schooled by those over there . . . so much so that I almost feel I'm there already.

Well, you certainly don't look as if you're here. You're far too solid for that. But seriously, I must say that my coming here was indeed a revelation to me. Because I had fairly strong fixed ideas about this after-death business. To me—I thought, well, when the body was put into Mother Earth, that was the end of me. Of course, I realise now that me — or I, if I should speak in the so-called correct English—that I was more than the body. The same as a lot of people said that the preface to my plays was more to the point and more important than the play itself.

That's quite true.

Oh, you agree with that, do you?

Oh, I do. I think your prefaces are marvellous.

Well, it's a pity they couldn't act the preface, and just leave the play out . . .

Well, just recently they can't even do the play.

What do you mean, "can't even do the play"? I admit one or two of my plays, like Shakespeare's, were more or less unactable. In fact there are still one or two of my plays that I have never yet seen acted. I've seen them 'put on'. I've seen them, so called, produced. And I've seen various members of the theatrical profession (God save the mark!) make an attempt at it.

But I suppose, after all, you couldn't blame them, because, after all, I must admit now that a lot of the characters I wrote were really puppets, for my own ideas and my own thoughts. Although I like sometimes to flatter myself that I did create some characters that had real life. And certainly I attempted to take them from life as I saw it, and people that I knew.

You had a wonderful insight into life . . .

Anyway, it's nice to know that they're jigging it up with a bit of music, isn't it?

What are your opinions of it?

I never condemn now. I used to do plenty of that when I was on earth, but I've learnt better; that it's a sin to condemn, and I've never been terribly keen to be a sinner. In fact, when I tried to be a sinner, I was never very successful—much to my great disappointment. I wanted to sin once or twice with several very charming ladies, but they would only sin by correspondence, which was no satisfaction to me at all!

Your correspondence with Ellen Terry, you know . . . I've read some of them . . .

Well, of course, if Ellen Terry had had any sense she'd have got rid of all those damn letters.

She did.

Oh, she did?

She would have, but . . .

But, of course, I kept a few, too. Still, I was a bit of a sentimental old fool, you know, but I wouldn't let people know it. At least, I tried to avoid them realising it. I used to put on a brusque manner, you know, and try and waggle my beard and frighten them. I didn't always succeed; I did it much better by postcards. Now I come to think about it, I was much more successful with my pen than ever I was with my tongue. Anyway, why are we talking in the past?

Well, I would love to know, G.B.S. (I know that's you, all right, by what you've said already) . . . When you were passing over . . . Tell us something about that. I'm always very interested . . .

I never knew a woman who was so anxious to know about death before! Why don't you wait until you come?

Oh, it's interesting to know . . .

Surely, my dear, it's more interesting to know something about life rather than death.

Yes, but then you can start with death, you see, and as you gradually go on, we will hear a bit more.

One usually starts with birth and ends up with death. But now I've had to reverse the procedure and start at death.

Well, it is really a birth, isn't it?

It is, of course. I'm merely being facetious.

Yes, I know. Just like you.

But I must admit that I was very much surprised, and very much perturbed . . . and at the same time very elated; if one can have three such different emotions all at once. I was elated because I realised that I hadn't lost the opportunity to do something which I'd always wanted to do—and that was write a successful play. Because you know although financially my plays were successful, I was never really satisfied with them myself. But I'm just telling you that as a secret. You must never let anyone else know. Otherwise they might think that I wasn't so good as they thought I was!

Where were we? Talking about life after death, and being reborn into a new world and . . . well, so many things happened all at once. Of course, I did meet, obviously, many dear friends of mine. Why they ever remained friends of mine, well, I never really know, not even to this day. Because, you know, when I come to think about it, I didn't always treat my friends as they treated me. But that's another story; we'll go into that some other time, because I believe that confession's good for the soul, providing you're not a Roman Catholic! Where were we?

I was talking about people that I met. Well, I met my own parents, of course. I can't say I was exactly elated about that, but they seemed to be much more excited about it than I was. But I did meet one or two people that I was very very attracted to, and very fond of. One of course was dear Pat; you know who I refer to—Patrick Campbell. Another was dear Ellen. . . . Another was Henry—I won't call him 'Sir', because there are no sirs over here. Another whom I was extremely drawn to in the earlier years of my life, who . . . Strangely enough we differed; but then again I've found since that the people I liked most were often the people I differed most with.

I suppose it was something because we were opposites, and they would stand up to me. And I always admired someone who stood up to me. I never could stand those craven fools that used to write me such long letters, and were afraid to come and beard the lion in the den. I always admired the man who had the nerve to walk up my front garden and knock at my door. I used to think to myself: Well, this man deserves to be let in—not that I always did, but still . . . The people who used to write long letters: I often answered them with a postcard, because I thought that was the best way out of it.

Where were we? Oh, I was talking about Oscar. Of course, you know he was a fool, but then again most of the best people are! Most of the most intellectual and brilliant people, as far as the world is concerned, are considered fools; so there's hope perhaps for you!

Oh, you were a great friend of Oscar's, were you?

In his earlier years: in my earlier years. I didn't always see eye to eye with him.

I have a great admiration for him.

Yes, I know. He was very much maligned, but of course he was a foolish young man nevertheless. Then there was that friend Bossey (Boysie) of his.

He was foolish as the world sees it. Is that right?

Well, when you're in the world you can be foolish to a point, but you must never let the world know too much. Actually, always keep the world guessing. They think much more of you.

Anyway, we are rather wandering off from Ayot St. Lawrence and other places connected with myself.

Do you ever visit there?

Oh, that place! Not now. I used to, but it seems rather like an empty shell. As a matter of fact, sometimes I've had a damn good laugh at some of the silly fools that go there. I respect them, mind you: don't misunderstand me. But, you know, that anyone should want to turn my house into a museum, and that anyone should expect to feel, or have any emotional reaction concerning myself, strikes me as being rather amusing; because I was not the type of person, I think, to command so much, shall we say, affection.

In fact, the only people, I think, who really had any affection for me were the children, who were never really frightened of me like the adults. I think children are much more trusting; they have much more faith in human beings. Whereas as you get older you become suspicious; and children are very rarely suspicious, especially of old men, because I think that they realise that old men might be Father Christmas in disguise, and bring them a nice present at Christmas if they treat them nicely.

Anyway, I think many a child round there thought I was probably Father Christmas dressed up like an ordinary old man all through the summer, and in the winter I donned a red coat and hat, and I went around on a sleigh. I probably would have filled the position very nicely, now I come to think of it. In fact I think I'd have made a much better Father Christmas than a playwright!

Oh, I don't know . . .

Well, perhaps not. I'm just joking; because I realise that you are in rather an invidious position, poor dears, sitting up here in this room in the dark, listening to a voice coming out of the void, and not knowing quite who, what or how. After all, I say I'm G.B.S. You haven't the faintest idea. I might be Jesus Christ for all you know. But there you are; that's a matter of opinion.

Oh, but we know you're G.B.S. by what you say.

But you know, when you come to think of it, people do accept things too much on face value. I realise, of course, that it is not always possible for people on this side to convince those on your side, especially if they are like poor Thomas, who was doubting, and wouldn't be satisfied until he'd put his hand in the side of Christ.

The point is that we have got to give conviction to the best of our ability. But sometimes, you know, it is not as easy as all that. Because many of us who would like to say certain things as evidence find it very embarrassing, because to do that we may have to involve or concern other people who perhaps wouldn't like to be tied up with we poor spirits.

And it's very difficult, too, when you consider all the barriers of religion. Most of my friends, or should I say a number of my closer acquaintances, were all so wrapped up with the Pope that you could never separate the two, you know.

You weren't a Roman Catholic, were you?

No, no, no. I was nothing. In my childhood I was linked with the Catholic Church; but as soon as I was able to think a little, I began to gently break the chains. But that doesn't mean to say that I haven't got every sympathy with Roman Catholics if they're sincere. But how they keep up with all these saints rather baffles me. And I don't quite know how all the saints keep up with the Roman Catholics. But probably they have some secret method of which I have not yet discovered the way it's done.

G.B.S., do you have plays over there?

Oh yes. And I still write, and I think I'm improving. I think I am definitely improving. And I'm hoping eventually to get over one or two that I think might be of some use in your poor emaciated theatre of today.

Isn't it dreadful?

Well, what little I've seen of it here and there is pretty appalling.

You're rather pleased you're where you are!

Well, I'm not sorry, but I can't say that I'm altogether glad either. That may sound a bit of a contradiction. I'm glad to be dead, and I'm very glad to be alive. At the same time, now I know what I know, I wish I were on earth so that I could write a few jolly good plays that would make people sit up and really take notice.

Oh, G.B.S., I wish you would write a play . . .

Well, who knows? Probably I will ma'am. Probably when you have your séances or meetings I may be permitted to come through occasionally, and, who knows, perhaps together we'll write a play.

Oh, that would be wonderful . . .

*And I know Oscar's very interested; and as for that
chappie friend of yours, Chopin, he's rounding us all up.*

Isn't he a wonderful soul, G.B.S.?

*He's a very fine fellow indeed; but you know there's
such a thing as letting the dead rest! And if I know him,
he's not going to let anybody rest!*

Oh, tell me a little about him, G.B.S.

*Of course, you're a fan worshipper, aren't you? What
they're termed in the modern sense. Because you're one
like the old days of the Wallerites. You were probably one
of the Kows.*

I was!

*I don't know what the theatre would do without hero
worshippers and fans.*

I wonder, do you know what is going to happen to the
theatre? They all seem to be pulled down, and I'm afraid
the cinema is going to take its place — the cinema and
television and so on. Because that would be a great pity,
G.B.S., wouldn't it?

*I don't think the theatre will ever completely die out,
but I must say it does need revitalising.*

It does! There are no real actors and actresses today.

*I don't think there are the artistes of the calibre of the
old days. I think that is partly because there are no great
actor-managers. I think it is that in the old days they used
to, as you know, tour the provinces; they used to learn
their work the hard way. I mean they were trained; they
knew every aspect of their art. They weren't fêted and
courted by society like they are today. Today the theatrical
profession seems more interested in the social register than
it actually seems interested in 'the boards', which I think
is a pity. You can't divide yourself. There are exceptions,
of course.*

*In Irving's latter days he was very much courted and
fêted; but he always kept his distance, more or less, from
the general public. But then again, I think that he had the
theatre at heart; he wanted to make it respectable because,*

you know, in my early years the theatre wasn't exactly a respectable place. No, it was the sort of place where one went to be entertained, and one admired the actors of the day.

One went to see special types of plays and special types of theatres; and the orchestra-pit was put there to separate the public from the vagabonds. That was the only reason that they ever had an orchestra-pit, because it wasn't particularly so much the musicians that mattered, because they were just put there with their instruments to keep the two apart. Usually somebody would blow on a trumpet to let people know there was a difference between the angels and the devils.

Anyway later on, of course, it became more respectable, more accepted, and society politely mingled with their gloves on. You know, of course, they wouldn't take their gloves off; I mean, that would never do. In my day, you know, the gentleman wore his white gloves, and the lady wore her white gloves right up to the elbow. It was a very polite society. In fact, if you wanted to blow your nose, you turned your back and you felt, if you could, for a handkerchief. If you didn't manage, then you wiped your nose on the back of your glove quietly, hoping no one knew. Those were the days when society was Society, in the time of Edward and Victoria.

There was little more in the communication. After two or three minutes the séance ended like this:—

I can't stay indefinitely. And in any case I've already had the warning.

G.B.S., are you outside or inside the body while you're talking?

What a peculiar question! I am inside the body as far as I know. Although actually I can't honestly say. Anyway I must go, and I must wish you good-night; and I'll come and talk to you again when possible.

In fact there was another communication from Shaw through Leslie Flint, but there was little of particular interest in it.

The 'warning' which is mentioned near the end of the tape probably refers to the failing of the power which enables the voice-box to function.

It is doubtful whether any Irish intonation is discernible in the communication. If this is indeed what it purports to be, the reason for the lack of an appropriate accent may be the artificial method of the production of the voice, as was suggested earlier. Apart from this, I remember what one of Shaw's friends told me, namely that the Irish accent was put on when he spoke on public occasions.

There is one particular question which I am often asked by someone who has listened to the tape-recording. Why, they say, didn't Mrs. Creet ask G.B.S. for details of the kind of life he was experiencing, as they themselves would have done?

For me, the answer is obvious. Although Mrs. Creet was very interested in the experiences of those who had just died; because of the great number of sittings she had had with Leslie Flint, her curiosity about the general nature of life after death had been exhausted.

In any case, Shaw seemed less concerned about providing an account of his present existence than in reminiscing about his former life.

SEVEN

The Nature of Life After Death

It ought to be emphasized that the *post-mortem* life which is described through psychic channels is only the first stage of future existence. It seems that when there is progression to 'higher spheres' experiences so unlike those of earth are encountered that they are beyond any attempt to describe them. But, even in the first stage, the indications of its nature that are given in the Shaw communication should not be taken as typical.

Bernard Shaw was a very remarkable man, and one of his characteristics was his skilful use of an impish humour to give point to profound problems. The tape-recording may give the impression that Shaw was finding his new life all a bit of a joke; but this impression I am sure would be a false one. It is just the Shavian treatment of a subject of tremendous importance.

It is a common criticism of the after-life that is depicted through mediumistic communications that our future existence would seem to be a very mundane affair — just a boring extension of our earthly life — and of course it is not only the G.B.S. tape that may seem to support this view.

Many psychic communications, particularly in the view of religious people, exhibit an extremely materialistic picture of 'the other side'. In part this may be due to the sort of question which most sitters put to their discarnate friends and relations. Their chief concern is that the latter are still alive and happy. They do not commonly ask 'religious' questions, probably because the great majority of those who go to séances are not much concerned with theological matters.

The first stage of life beyond death seems material, in the sense that conditions are described which approximate to earthly circumstances, although this kind of experience is said to be temporary and to last only until a higher spiritual state is attained. But even during this first phase there is evidence, if the right questions are asked, that religious experience is far from lacking.

Sometimes those who speak in Leslie Flint's séances express strong religious opinions. Shaw mentioned a Dr. Charles Marshall who helped him to speak. Dr. Marshall himself often spoke at sittings and, twice at least when I was present, at some length. The second occasion was concerned with medical matters, but the first was entirely devoted to religion. Here are some extracts from what was said, in response initially to a question which I asked:

A.B. In your new life have you any greater knowledge of God than you had before?

C.M. *When you ask me if I have a greater knowledge, I suppose in a sense I should say No, and yet there is an answer that could be given when I say Yes. Shall we say that one has a better consciousness of God, a greater realisation of God. The whole point is, it's a matter of emotional feeling . . . God is to us a mighty force of power, of which we are much more conscious than any of you can possibly hope to be while upon earth. Certainly we know God; not in the physical sense, but in a mental and spiritual one.*

Dr. Marshall was critical of the Church. Later on in our talk he said:—

It seems to me that the Church has lost the way, for the simple reason it has failed to follow the Prince of Peace, the man who had nowhere to lay his head. The Church is much more concerned with power—much more concerned with material things than spiritual things. By that I do not mean to say that there are not sincere people in the Church, people who are members of the Church—there are many— but I am afraid the Church as a body is a very materialistic thing in comparison to the simple man Jesus.

When I mentioned the emphasis which the Church places upon corporate worship, the following comment was made:—

Although it may be very pleasant and very nice to gather together to worship—and certainly it is a good thing if it is sincere—I cannot help feeling that religion is something that must be lived. In other words, you must express God's love and will through your life. To me that is the thing that matters. To me that is religion; it is the religion—to give forth Christ, to give forth God's will and love through service, through yourself.

I know many and many a person—at least I did on earth, and I still know from this side—many a person who never went in a church from the time they were in Sunday School or something who, believe me, were far, infinitely far, better Christians, and more worthy to be called Christians, than many a person who stands up in a pulpit.

To those who feel the need, I say, "Go to church". But I suppose you must also remember that I was a doctor, and when one's a doctor one sees so much, perhaps more than many. One goes to many who are in great need—not only physically, believe me, but spiritually. And when one has seen many people pass from your world to this, and tried to relieve suffering as one does as a doctor, one sees many aspects and angles, and one realises that the people are crying out in your world for truth; they're crying out for comfort in the hour of need.

The Church should preach what we are endeavouring to give to you. The Church has failed utterly in this. In fact the Church, as I see it, is a miserable failure. Why is it that you come here? Why is it that your Church, for instance, hasn't taught you this—hasn't given you the conviction you are seeking? What is wrong with your Church that you should have to seek this truth outside it? Something is sadly lacking. Christ demonstrated it; the early disciples demonstrated it.

The early Christians for many many years demonstrated these things. That's why they had the fervour of their conviction. They didn't care if they had to go into the arena. I say they didn't care. In a physical sense they did; they were still human. But they had that strong religious fervour that this Kingdom of God was at hand: that when the physical body had passed they would be released from it and be in the Kingdom of God. They had such wonderful faith. As I see it, the Church does not give that faith any more. It certainly doesn't demonstrate it. If this truth were brought into the Church in a true sense, it would revolutionise it. The churches would be full throughout the world. The Church offers those who mourn a stone. That's why I'm a little impatient with the Church: it does not do its duty.

When Dr. Marshall says that trying to follow the example of Christ is of greater importance than attendance at church services, he is only stating the obvious, as the clergy of all churches would agree, although they might stress that being a member of the local worshipping community is a necessary part of religious life.

But the chief reason for Dr. Marshall's censure of the Church is that it does not emphasize the entry into a new life after death and provide evidence of this. I cannot share his optimism that if this were done the churches worldwide would be full; but it is true, I think, that the Church does neglect its doctrine of eschatology—the teaching about death and what follows it.

These are not popular religious subjects today. It is natural enough that we human beings, although aware of our mortality, should think about it as little as possible. Until comparatively recent times, most people were not infrequently confronted with the sight of the process of dying. Today, when most deaths take place in hospital rather than in the family, it is not brought to so many people's attention as was the case in former generations.

Anything to do with death is banished from thought as far as possible. And this is not simply because the subject is an unpleasant one: it is also because, for so many people, there is no conviction that there is anything the other side of it.

Even those who still have a strong conviction that there is a life beyond death may have less definite opinions than they had formerly about God reviewing their previous earthly existence and finally decreeing punishment or reward.

The majority of religious people nowadays think of God as a God of mercy rather than of judgement. Since Freud, the idea of severe punishment for wrongdoing has become unfashionable, and most Christians would agree that the conception of God casting a sinner into eternal torment is completely unacceptable.

But a minority of those who profess the Christian faith still teach that the wicked will be cast into hell. This view tends to be held by those at opposite ends of the theological spectrum. Certainly there are those of the extreme fundamentalist sects who believe that the 'unsaved' face an eternity of suffering. And Roman Catholics, so far removed from these sects in their theology, are popularly thought to have a similar belief.

I have considerable doubts about this reflecting the position of most Roman Catholics. A few years ago, one of their theologians, a priest who was well known because he was a frequent broadcaster, was the speaker at a meeting which I attended. He was an unusual representative of his church inasmuch as he believed that his father, who had died, communicated with him—directly, I should add: not through a medium.

When question time came, and there was a discussion about life after death, I asked the speaker what would happen if someone died in mortal sin. Without a moment's hesitation he said, "He would go to hell." Then he added, with a gentle smile, "But, so far as we know, nobody has gone there yet!"

What has psychic evidence got to say about this subject? I think that it supports a middle view. It suggests that there may well be suffering after death, depending on the nature of previous earthly life, but that this suffering is only temporary, although sometimes protracted.

One activity in which many Spiritualists are engaged is participation in the activities of what are popularly called

'Rescue Circles'. These consist usually of only a small number of people—say half a dozen or so—one of whom is a trance medium.

The theory underlying the work of these groups is that the medium in trance becomes the vehicle of communication between those who have died and the members of the circle. But the communications are not of a general nature; they have a specific purpose. Their aim is to help those who find themselves in difficulties of one kind or another in their new *post-mortem* life — to 'rescue' them from the unhappy conditions in which they find themselves.

It is not only those in trouble who speak through the medium. There is also the discarnate 'guide' who is in charge of the proceedings, and other enlightened spirits whose responsibility it is to bring those to be rescued to talk, by means of the medium, to those who are waiting to help them.

This help consists in explaining to their communicators the reasons for the unhappiness and confusion which they are experiencing, and in showing them a way of escape from their misfortune.

If the evidence is to be believed, the majority, perhaps, of those who are brought to talk to the circle are not even aware that they have died. This, in itself, is a cause of confusion and distress, and a simple clarification of their state may resolve their difficulty. When they have been convinced that they are dead—but alive in another existence—all they may need is advice as to how, in their new world, they may find those who will help them to make progress to a happier state of being.

If the question is asked, Why cannot these discarnate helpers make themselves known to those in need of their help without the efforts of the rescue circle, the answer is given that the confused and distressed spirits are nearer the earth, as it were, than the next world, and cannot see or hear those who live in it, until it has been explained to them by the members of the circle how the necessary new sight and hearing may be attained.

But the confused state may not be a solitary one. There may be others present who have also died. There may be figments of the imagination—people and places, pleasant or otherwise—which appear to be completely real and substantial.

It is, indeed, this apparent reality and 'earthiness' of the surroundings which has caused the one who has died not to suspect his condition. In addition, it is usually found that he has experienced a sudden and unexpected death. Someone who has died after a long illness will probably not be so misled.

Those in quite different stages of moral progress may find themselves in this *post-mortem* state of confusion, but, as might be expected, the lot of the comparatively good man or woman is different from that of the comparatively evil one.

EIGHT

Norman Hunt
and his Rescue Circle

When somebody, through the help of the rescue circle, has been brought to the realisation of his state, it may not be possible for him to make progress towards happier circumstances until, to use religious language, he repents; until, that is, he faces up to the wrong he has done in his former life and feels sincere remorse about it. This can be an extremely painful process, and, inasmuch as no man or woman is by any means completely good, everyone when he dies must, at some stage, come to terms with his earthly misdoings.

An illustration of this is provided by the case of Alf Higgins, a soldier who, with some companions, was killed by a shell during the first world war. He was helped by the rescue circle whose leader was Norman Hunt. An extract from a tape-recording of one visit of Alf to the circle—after he had found happiness in his new life—is given below: but first let me say something about Norman Hunt and his group.

For about eleven years this group met regularly every week, and carefully tape-recorded the proceedings. Mr. Hunt told me that some twenty-five miles of tape resulted, and that a hundred or more people from 'the other side' had talked with them. The circle broke up about twenty years ago, when the medium, Walter Rickard, left Tunbridge Wells, where the meetings were held, to live in another part of England. I ought to mention that Rickard was not a professional medium, and no money was involved in the series of meetings.

Both Mr. Hunt and Mr. Rickard are now dead, and most of the tapes are not available, as the lady to whom they were entrusted—a member of the circle—will not allow them to be inspected. However, Mr. Hunt made copies for me of the more interesting rescue cases, and among these is the case of

Alf. It is not possible to reproduce in print the Cockney accent which is so evident in the tape-recording, and which sounds so convincing to someone like myself who grew up in London after the 1914-1918 war. The medium was not a Cockney, and one of the fascinating aspects of this rescue circle's work is the multiplicity of accents and dialects with which their communicators spoke.

I remember playing some of Alf's communication to Jack Pizzey, the television presenter, in his office a good many years ago. He was so intrigued with it that, there and then, he telephoned his wife, Erin Pizzey (who is renowned for her work for battered wives), and, placing my tape-recorder close to the telephone, let her listen to part of the story.

The 'Mr. Abu' of whom Alf speaks is the guide who was the prime mover in all the activities of the circle. The tape-recording begins with Alf describing what happened when he and the other soldiers were killed. Two members of the group, Norman Hunt and John, made occasional comments.

*Alf   Got any questions for me, guv'nor? You was going to
  try and think up a question. If you ain't got no questions..*
N.H. I do know of one, Alf.
Alf   Do you, guv'nor? One what I could 'andle, eh?
N.H. Yes, I think so.
Alf   Good.
N.H. I'll ask it straight away, so we don't . . .
Alf   I'll be glad. I don't want to waste no time tonight.
N.H. All right. What I was going to ask you, Alf, was this.
  You were talking to us, you remember, about the people
  who 'had to think'.
Alf   Yes, guv'nor; what I was telling you about.
N.H. Yes. Well, can you remember, from your own
  experience, perhaps, or from what you've seen, what first
  starts that feeling that you've now got to think? Because,
  you see, up to a certain point you're not doing so. What
  makes you feel, "I must think. I must think"? Can you
  give me any ideas about that?

Alf　It ain't nothing what you knows of as starts it, guv'nor. Whether there might be some kind of influence . . . . 'Cause since I've been up 'ere, I know, like you know and all, as 'ow there's a lot of influencing going on what we don't know nothing about . . .

N.H.　That's true, of course.

Alf　So whether it was because there was some kind of a influencing going on what I never knew nothing about, or whether it was just as it 'appened, I wouldn't know, not now. But then, like I told you, it was all right. We was out of all the mess and all the trouble and that—'appy enough, quiet enough—looking for a boozer . . . . One of 'em says, "Look! See that there light?" Remember? Like I told you.

N.H.　Yes, I do.

Alf　Now, there, guv'nor, was a meeting. That was a meeting like what I was talking about to you last time when the new blokes was here.

N.H.　Yes, I know.

Alf　That was the meeting, guv'nor. That there light was a big un, see? What I never knew at the time. I turn me heyes off it, guv'nor: I wouldn't go—not with this 'ere bloke what did go. So I could 'ave been met; see guv'nor? 'Cause you've got your choice. If you don't want to be met, you don't 'ave to. You can send 'em away.

N.H.　Yes.

Alf　You can send 'em away. . . And I done it, and the others what was with me, done it and all. "Light? Can't see no light. Must be crackers—you know. Let 'im go." All right! Well, that was the one what was met, and we could all 'ave been met, similar, see?

N.H.　Yes, I understand you.

Alf　And you might say 'elped to be put right 'fore we was put right, in a way. Well, we knocked about—talking about me now—we knocked about, doing this, that and the other. Finding out as 'ow things was a bit strange. Settling ourselves down in this 'ere new kind of place, and wondering what about some leave; and when do we get 'ome to blighty; and what about the old woman. Because it was all earth thoughts you see, guv'nor. None of us, only this 'ere one what see the light, and what 'ad a little idea. None of the rest of us 'adn't got no ideas at all. So we was lost you might say, in a way. Because there wasn't no Company Officer to report to. There weren't no Sergeant-Major. Well, that was nice at times, you know! Ha ha! Didn't get ordered about; could do what we liked, see? And we done it, see? Very life-like you might say.

I tell you, we looked for a boozer. Well, all right, we find a boozer. We 'ave a drink; we 'ave a fag. It 'appened like that there. It goes on for quite a while. No occasion for thinking; only about the strangeness, you might say, of this 'ere new place. 'Ow long, I can't say; I told you before, I can't say. I just can't think in time, not no'ow. But I reckon it must 'ave been a goodish kind of time; and it would depend on 'ow soon you starts doing this 'ere thinking, 'ow long you stays where you are.

But the first thing that began to 'appen to me, guv'nor, was I begin to wonder. It wasn't a thinking like the sort of thinking what I told you about. It was just a beginning to wonder. A scratching me 'ead like and thinking, "Funny about this 'ere." A bit funny you know. Because this 'ere bloke what went off to the light what 'e spoke about, see: 'e said, "I know what's the matter with us. We're dead, and I'm going to see about this 'ere light." 'Course, we all laughed at 'im and said, "Dead? You might be dead; we ain't!" Well, I begin to wonder. I think to meself, "It's funny any'ow. Can't be dead, because this ain't being dead. On the other 'and, where's the Sergeant-Major and all on 'em?" See? "And the crowd. What's 'appened?"

What 'ad 'appened? I dunnow. Wish I could get 'old of somebody what could tell me. That was 'ow it started. Who could I get 'old of what could tell me; see? I thinks to meself, Well, I dunnow. Supposing as 'ow we was dead; supposing we was, who'd be the bloke to ask about it? Parson, I suppose. Parson's supposed to know all about

*that there. Course I never knew nothing in them days.
I dunnow, I thinks to meself, I'll 'ave to get this right.
'Cause, after all, you walk from one place to another—for
nothing, you know. You don't meet nobody what you
know, only the crowd what's a-knocking about there, and
they mean nothing to yer.*

*And then you 'ave a bit of a pause, you know. You'd
like to meet some of yer old mates. And then you begin to
wonder like I done. Mind you, I don't say as 'ow it 'appens
with everybody the same. I reckon it's different with
different people, but that's 'ow it 'appened to me. If now,
guv'nor, I'd 'ad a little idea—not so much as what you got,
but just a little idea; what you've told people what's come
'ere and spoke through other ladies; spoke through my
bloke to you and all.*

*If I'd 'ad a little idea like what you'd give them, when
they've been a-wondering and doing their a-thinking, you've
said to them; Look, when you get out of 'ere—'cause I've
'eard you; I'm interested in it—When you get out of 'ere,
you've said, You 'oller out for somebody; and you give
'em a name maybe.*

*All right, guv'nor. Now, if I'd 'ad that little idea, or if
I'd been lucky enough, you might say, to come into one of
these 'ere dos with people what's got sense like you 'ave,
what would 'ave told me that there, I would 'ave done it;
because what did I want, guv'nor, when I was all on me
own, wondering and a-thinking and a-worrying; because I
never knew 'ow I was ever going to get out of where I was,
see? Never knew 'ow. Then I would 'ave sent up this 'ere
'oller, like, wiv Donald, you know, and, like, wiv the other,
'Arild, 'im; sending out a 'oller.*

*And I'd 'ave got 'elp, because I'd turned me eyes that
there way, like what you've told them to do, and sent out
a 'oller. I never knew. I never knew.*

*I 'ave to wait, guv'nor, and I did wait. I wasn't un'appy
but I wasn't getting nowhere. And I wasn't proper 'appy: I
couldn't be. I was 'alf way in between, guv'nor. I wasn't in*

'eaven and I wasn't in 'ell, and I wasn't on earth. I wasn't nowhere, see what I mean? And that's what wasn't satisfying. It wasn't satisfying. So I 'ave to wait, guv'nor, till one of the blokes what I'm knocking about with, what's been doing 'is own bit of thinking—and that was our old friend, Frenchie—'e sends out a 'oller.

'E gets somebody come down, you know who, to give 'im 'elping 'and. 'E goes on up wiv 'er. I decides to go along wiv 'em. That's 'ow it come about.

Then I come up 'ere. Then you tell me as 'ow it was thirty-five year. Well, all right, it don't matter; it don't matter. It don't matter. It ain't only over 'ere as it don't matter. Look back yerself over yer own lifetime on the earth. When did that there 'appen, you thinks to yerself. That were fifteen year ago, that were. It don't matter, do it guv'nor?

N.H. Not a bit.

Alf Well, it's just the same; it's just the same. The condition, yus, the condition; that's what I've always said when I've 'ad a chance to talk about these 'ere kind of things. Yus, the condition, but not the time.

N.H. No. Quite right.

Alf I said; I forget who it was; I said, I think it was the other lady; "Don't be sorry for 'em about the time. Be sorry for 'em about the condition." Because while the condition is there, guv'nor, it's all the time there is. There ain't going to be no other time, see. And you can't say, I was there thirty-five years; I was un'appy three times longer than the bloke what was there only ten years. It ain't like that. I can't explain it; it's the condition.

Well, that's 'ow it come about, guv'nor. Mind you, I wasn't—I know now—I wasn't a wicked one, you know. No, I wasn't, guv'nor. I couldn't 'ave been or I wouldn't 'ave been where I was. But I wouldn't like to 'ave been, now I know a bit more. Because where I wasn't un'appy there's them what is. And they're 'arder to get out, unless they can be brung along to people like you.

N.H. And even then it's hard sometimes.

Alf Even then, guv'nor, it's 'ard sometimes. Yus; but that's 'ow it worked out. And about the thinking side of it which you was talking about; that's 'ow it started with me. What did I think about? Well, I 'ad plenty of time. And you keep an 'old of yer memory, guv'nor. You keep a tight 'old on yer memory; you don't lose nothing when you come over 'ere. On the other 'and it's a bit clearer.

And when you've got all the time, and there ain't nothing else what you've got to do, and there ain't nothing else what comes to yer; it don't matter 'ow long yer takes to think about the things what yer got to think about. And you've got to think about them.

John You've got nothing else to do, really.

Alf Of course you ain't, John boy; that's what it comes down to. That's what it comes down to. By the time I'd done wandering about, enjoying not being in the mud; enjoying no Sergeant-Major, and all that there: by the time that was finished there wasn't nothing else; nothing to do.

John All these people who have been brought to us had that one thing in common. As you say, not necessarily unhappy, but they are unsatisfied.

Alf Yes, that's it, John boy. That's it, John boy. That's what starts you on the thing.

John They won't always admit it . . . .

Alf Oh, you can tell it; you can tell it in their faces. I've told the guv'nor; you can tell it in their faces, what they've been through: course you can. Well, they think, same as what I think, if there's something or other what's at the back of yer mind, yer might say, as yer think, "Well, I don't know; I don't think I'll think about that there one; it ain't nice to think about." You know, it might be something unpleasant, see? You don't 'ave to; all right, but you stay where you are till you do.

And you've got all the time, all the time, and there you stay till you do. And you get it straight with yerself; with yerself. I can't give no other explanation. I never 'ad to go to no church. I never 'ad to do nothing. I never 'ad to say I was sorry, not to nobody . . . only meself. There's where them remorses come in; see guv'nor? You burn it out, like that there.

And if you've got a lot to burn out, well, get on with it, you got to do it: you got to do it. Only, like me, most of 'em just don't know, guv'nor. They don't know. They ain't even got the idea. That's why I'm glad to be able to 'elp Mister Abu—and you—a little bit, by doing my little share of our job.

N.H. Indeed, you do.

Alf   Just like that. There's people over 'ere, 'undreds and thousands of 'em, what ain't interested. They've been through the same as what I 'ave, and worse, 'undreds and 'undreds and 'undreds of 'em. They're contented, they're satisfied, they're 'appy with the life what they find now— what they've earned; 'cause you don't come 'ere unless it's right. They've cleaned up their little lot: see what I mean, guv'nor? They've done their thinking, and that's brung 'em up 'ere. That's brung 'em up 'ere. All right, they're satisfied. They don't feel no urge, you might say, to come back 'ere on the earth and talk to people. It's all right; it don't matter, yer don't 'ave to, yer don't 'ave to.

But I couldn't get over it, guv'nor; I couldn't get over it when I talked to my girl Eileen what brung me up 'ere, second 'and you might say: it wasn't special for me—and all the better for that. I talked it over wiv 'er: I knew she was 'anging about close to the earth, and she told me why.

I says to 'erself, "Well, now, look, my girl"—'cause I calls 'er my girl same as what I do call my girl 'ere, see. "Now, look, my girl," I says, "It means as 'ow there's a lot of people coming over, like what I done, what don't know nothing about it: and they're going to be in the same old mess as what I'm in unless we can do something about telling 'em. Now, 'ow can we tell 'em, see?" Well, of course, 'ere's the answer, guv'nor.

My girl says, "If you feel like that there, Alf, there's a chance for a little job. There's a job waiting for you, see?" That's what started me 'ere, guv'nor. Mind yer, the orders might 'ave come from further up. I dunno. But that's 'ow it passes on to me. That's 'ow it passes on to me. It's only now wiv talking wiv you people, and listening to what Mister Abu 'ave to say, and all that, as 'ow I 'ave realised as 'ow there is orders what comes from up top.

And this 'ere thinking thing very likely started off with an influencing from somebody what I never knew about. Might be: might be. I reckon it was, now I know more. Well, that's 'ow it worked.

N.H. Well, thank you for that little talk, Alf. That's very interesting, I find. Very.

Alf   Now I can think, over 'ere where I am. And I've cleaned up all the darker side of it, guv'nor, and got it straight wiv meself. I've been through me little bits of remorse and that . . . . If I 'adn't I wouldn't be 'ere where I am. And now I can think—and I can think on the 'appier side. Instead of thinking of the nipper what I give a clip round the ear 'ole, I can think of the one what I give a penny to. And it gives you a little warm feeling, guv'nor, see?

Guv'nor, I don't want to get all sloppy, but when you get 'ere, guv'nor, and yer finds yer can *think that there way, and you ain't got to think about the other way 'cause you've* done *yer thinking about that there—it rams 'ome this 'ere love, guv'nor, that's what it do. Because this 'ere God—I don't know nothing about 'im—God bless 'im, I don't know nothing about 'im. 'E's God to me, and it's good enough. Mister Abu knows all about 'im, maybe.*

N.H. No; I don't think so!

Alf   Well, a lot, guv'nor, 'cause 'e do talk to you a lot about God, and God being love and that. I don't pretend to know about the words and all that . . . . it don't matter. But this 'ere God, guv'nor, 'ave said to me; and 'e 'ave said to everybody what's got 'ere; and 'e will say to everybody

*what ain't got 'ere yet, but will: and 'e'll say to you people
if you find yourself in the same position.*

*'E'll pat yer on the 'ead, guv'nor, and 'e'll say, "That's
all right. You got it square. Now then, get on with it. If
you got a little job to do, best of luck; get on with it. You
can be 'appy now. You've worked it out for yourself.
You've worked it out for yourself, with a little 'elp, yes;
but you've done it yourself."*

*You've got to do it yourself. Nobody else can't do
your thinking for you. And it rams 'ome this 'ere love
of God, guv'nor, like nothing else can. Because, you see,
we're a-living in it. Not like Mister Abu, maybe. I reckon
'e's 'appier than what I know 'ow to be: but never mind,
I'm 'appy enough. And we're a-living in it.*

I can imagine many of those who read Alf's account of
his after-death experiences expressing considerable doubt
about the possible truth of it: and certainly to a member of
a Christian church it may appear not only ludicrous but also
theologically unorthodox. I would remind such a person of
what was said of Gordon Burdick by Canon Pearce-Higgins.
We must not expect too much in the way of theological
expertise from those who have died. They may know no
more after death than they did before, although it is to be
hoped that enlightenment will be gained in due course.

Alf claimed no knowledge of God. Obviously he would
not have called himself a Christian, except, it might be, in
the most nominal sense. He would have little understanding
about the Atonement, for example, and would have had no
difficulty in accepting the theory that each human being had
to work out his or her own salvation.

I believe, myself, that there is much misunderstanding
about the meaning of the doctrine of the Atonement, and
that it does not absolve the repentant sinner from the results
of his wrong-doing. What it does, in my interpretation of it, is
to restore the sinner to a proper relationship with God. That
is to say, it is an 'At-one-ment'.

Wrong done on earth will cause suffering to the wrong-doer, here or hereafter, although the suffering may be only that of real remorse; but the outcome will be a realisation of the love of God, and a right relationship with Him. And that is what Alf seemed to experience, however unorthodox his description of the experience may appear.

If I am right about this, Alf may have already reached a considerable degree of enlightenment.

NINE

What Did Jesus Teach ?

Before I go on to give further examples from Mr. Hunt's tapes, I should like to devote a few pages to the consideration of what Christians are taught about their religion, and whether this reflects what Jesus taught.

Let us suppose that in India a man who is literate, but has no knowledge of the Christian faith, finds a copy of the earliest of the Gospels, St. Mark, printed in a language which he knows.

What sort of impression of Jesus and his teaching would the contents of St. Mark's Gospel make upon someone completely ignorant of Christianity, who reads it for the first time? The reason why I have given this Gospel as an example is because St. Mark is regarded by scholars as the Gospel which most clearly reflects what Jesus taught. These scholars do not of course believe that every word of this Gospel is true. There was no one among the disciples of Jesus who wrote down the words which he spoke. What we find in the Gospels came to their authors from what the disciples or others remembered about Jesus, or what they had been told about him; and (unless we believe in literal verbal inspiration) these memories would not always be word-for-word correct. In addition to this, those who edited the Gospels sometimes may have made mistakes, or deliberately have made alterations, omissions or additions. Also, those who made copies of the Gospels no doubt themselves made a certain number of errors.

Nevertheless, St. Mark's Gospel probably gives us the best picture we can obtain of the teaching of Jesus and what he was like. It is not a chronological account of his life—it is not a biography in the modern sense. Like the 'lives' of the saints, it is a collection from different sources of stories about a venerated figure.

Read St. Mark, trying to forget all that you know about the Christian faith. Try to put yourself in the place of the man I have mentioned. If he sits down to read it, what sort of impression of Jesus and his message would he get?

One thing is certain. A great deal of the Gospel he would not understand. He would not fully understand, for example, the reason for the hostility which the Jewish religious establishment showed towards Jesus, and his reaction to that hostility. Some knowledge of Jewish history is necessary for that. He would not understand many of the parables of Jesus. He would not understand that most Christians equate Jesus with God. Indeed, at first sight, it might be difficult to see what of importance he would learn from St. Mark, which it must be remembered was written for early Jewish Christians in order to preserve knowledge of the earthly life of Jesus, whom ever since the resurrection they had been claiming as the Messiah.

Our hypothetical reader of St. Mark would notice that those who listened to Jesus were extremely impressed by his teaching, because, unlike the experts of the Jewish religious law, "he taught them as one with authority." It was obvious that he had great spiritual insight, and it seemed that he knew the mind of God in a way that contemporary religious leaders did not.

He never claimed to be equal with God, but he did call Him 'Father'.

Sometimes he is referred to as the Son of God or the Messiah. What the uninstructed reader would make of these terms it is impossible to say with any certainty. What is certain is that they would not suggest the Godhead.

Jesus, as shown in St. Mark's Gospel, is clearly subordinate to his heavenly Father. For example, in chapter 9, verse 37, he is reported as saying, "Whoever receives one of these children in my name receives me; and whoever receives me, receives not me but the One who sent me." And this idea of Jesus being sent by God, his Father, into the world with a mission occurs time after time in the Gospel. This mission was to proclaim the Kingdom of God.

But what would our reader understand by this term? As he read the Gospel I think he would come to realise that the Kingdom of God meant the will of God—who was love—operating in the hearts of men and women. What was the will of a loving God in respect of human conduct, according to St. Mark?

From what Jesus said, it was clear that God's will did not operate in the Jewish hierarchy, which ignored the divine laws. Outward practices and ceremonies had taken the place of spiritual truths, and earthly rank and wealth were given a position in religion which they did not merit. Above all, self-satisfaction and pride were endemic among the religious leaders.

Jesus said he had not come to those who, mistakenly, considered they lived exemplary lives, but to those spiritually sensitive people who knew they were sinners; those whose lives had in them much of which they were ashamed. To them he said, your lives will be changed for the better—you will find a new joy in them—if you live in accordance with the will of God, my Father.

This involved loving God and one's neighbour; that is, anybody with whom one came into contact. Life should be simple; greatness should be measured in terms of service to others. Prayer, when real, was very powerful, and its potential was unlimited.

The life of Jesus, as we find it in the Gospel, was in accordance with what he taught. He practised what he preached. By the manner of his life he showed to man what God was like: the son expressed the nature of his Father, so far as human nature was capable of this. As much emphasis is placed upon his remarkable ministry of compassionate healing as upon his teaching. He had no fixed home. With a few followers he travelled the country, spreading the 'good news', or Gospel. He foresaw the result of his teaching. The religious leaders would increasingly become opposed to him and finally would have him executed. But he would 'rise again three days afterwards'.

There are some people who claim that their lives have been changed — that they have been 'converted' — simply by reading the Gospel. It may be that the Gospel can act as a trigger, or perhaps a catalyst, for someone who, unconsciously, is prepared for this change: someone who is dissatisfied not only with his own life, but also with the traditional and ceremonial nature of his religion. Or someone who realises the emptiness of a life devoted to earthly ambition and desires.

Also, of course, Jesus teaches that man is a spiritual being and, as such, has a destiny stretching far beyond this life; and that this destiny is influenced by conduct here and now. This indeed is 'good news' for those who have believed that life is circumscribed by their short span of existence in this world, and that their ethical and spiritual growth would be cut short at death.

Now let us suppose that a man, ignorant of Christianity, who has become convinced of the truth of what Jesus taught, after reading St. Mark's Gospel, is taken to Rome or Canterbury during some great religious occasion in one of those cities. He might visit St. Peter's in Rome during a special Mass celebrated by the Pope, or he might be present at the enthronement of a new Archbishop of Canterbury. He would be astonished by what he saw. In a magnificent building he would witness a complicated ceremony conducted by extravagantly dressed priests who, if he could understand what they said, would convince him that they regarded Jesus as God, the Saviour of the world through the sacrifice of himself on the Cross for mankind.

All religions, of course, change and develop during the process of history, but the development of a religion is by no means always for the better: rather the reverse is liable to be the case. The founders of the great world religions, if they returned to earth today, could seldom behold with satisfaction what their followers had made of their teaching. The insight of great souls is obscured and misinterpreted by lesser men, and Christianity cannot expect to be an exception.

I am not suggesting that Christendom—and in particular that part which calls itself Catholic—has become corrupt and debased, or that popes and archbishops have not had good and humble men among them; men of simple life, trying earnestly to follow the example that was set nearly two thousand years ago. What I am venturing to suggest is that there has been a drastic transformation of the original Gospel which the apostles and others heard from the lips of Jesus.

Some of this transformation has been brought about by the weakness of human nature; by good intentions being overcome by the more animal component of man's make-up. This is the kind of change from which all religion suffers, and to which I have referred above. But there is reason to believe something of which most Christians are almost completely ignorant; and that is that their religion radically changed its course immediately after its beginning.

Christian theology, as distinct from the Christian religion, could be said to begin with St. Paul. Paul did not, of course, formulate a complete system of theology, but it was largely upon his writings in the New Testament that the theologians of later generations built their theories about the nature of Jesus, his relationship with the Father, and the significance of his death. These and related subjects, including the idea of a Holy Trinity, were hotly debated among the leaders of the Church before the orthodox doctrines, as we know them, emerged in the fourth and fifth centuries.

It is not realised, I think, by Christians generally how Paul dominates so much of the New Testament. For Christians this is by far the most important element of the Bible, and it may be divided, so far as the length of text is concerned, into two roughly equal parts—the four Gospels and everything else that comes after them. The second part is largely concerned with the life of Paul. Nearly two-thirds of the Acts of the Apostles is devoted to what he said and did, and the great majority of the Epistles are attributed to him. It is likely that the Gospels themselves did not escape his influence, as St. Luke was his faithful physician and companion in missionary endeavour.

What a person believes depends, to a greater or lesser degree, upon the kind of person he is; and so the character of Paul is of some importance. From what we read about him in the New Testament, it is evident that he was dominantly male in a way that most modern men are not. This was, no doubt, because he was a Jew, and Jews of his period generally did not have a high opinion of women, who were thought to be an inferior creation compared with men.

There are certain predominant male characteristics—both good and bad—and other predominant female ones, but they are not mutually exclusive. For example, men are usually more aggressive than women: women are more gentle than men. But the average man can be gentle on occasion, and most women can sometimes be aggressive. It is a matter of degree. Paul seems to have been unusually deficient in the distinctively womanly virtue of compassion, which was so conspicuous in the life of Jesus, in whom male and female virtues appear to find a perfect balance.

The thirteenth chapter of I Corinthians is a marvellous dissertation upon love in its Christian sense, and describes this virtue in a way that can seldom have been surpassed. But this virtue was not expressed perfectly in Paul's own life—nor could this reasonably be expected. He never claimed to live completely in accord with what he taught. Paul never asserted that he lived a perfect life: he had human failings like all the rest of us, but there is no doubt that he had the attributes necessary for bringing his new religion into the Gentile world.

No one would dispute the vital part that Paul played in the growth and expansion of the early Church, but the question must be asked, did he preach the Gospel as Jesus had taught it? As I have mentioned above, his character must have had some influence upon his interpretation of the Faith; and in spite of I Corinthians 13, a certain hardness—a lack of compassion—is observable in some of his speeches and sermons.

But of much greater importance, theologically speaking, is the origin of his knowledge of Jesus and his teaching. Paul was insistent that he had received this knowledge, not, like other contemporary converts, from those who had known Jesus, or indeed from any earthly source, but from Jesus himself after the completion of his earthly life. In other words, he believed that, on occasion, he was in direct communication with the risen Lord, who instructed him in matters of faith and behaviour.

Paul's sincerity in this belief is not in question, but was this communication—supposing it took place—influenced by certain contents of his unconscious mind? There is evidence in psychical research that this can happen in the case of communications of a psychical nature — in telepathy for example — and while there may be distaste in applying the term 'psychical' in the case of Paul, there is little doubt that he had certain experiences which we might call psychic. In II Corinthians, 12, for example, he writes, "I shall go on to tell of visions and revelations granted by the Lord."

If Paul's teaching about Jesus, as we find it in Acts and the Epistles, corresponded with that of Peter and the rest of the apostles who formed in Jerusalem the first Christian community, this question concerning the reliability of the visions would be of little importance. But the fact is that the teaching of Paul appears to differ in certain respects from that of the earliest Christian Church.

On the day of Pentecost, according to Acts 2, after the reception of the Holy Spirit, Peter, supported by the rest of the Eleven, addressed the crowd of people who had been listening in astonishment to the apostles speaking 'in tongues'. In this first Christian sermon, as it may be described, Peter refers to Jesus as "a man singled out by God and made known to you through miracles, portents and signs". He refers to "the resurrection of the Messiah" which had been foretold in the Old Testament.

Peter taught that those who accepted Jesus as the Messiah should repent and be baptised in his name for the remission of sins; that they would then receive the Holy Spirit and be enabled to amend their lives. Beyond death there would be personal life after God's judgement. There was nothing in the early teaching of the apostles of the divinity of Jesus, or that belief in him would result in salvation — "the saving of man from the power and penalty of sin," as the dictionary puts it.

But Paul, in his teaching, provided the basis for a new idea, the doctrine of the Vicarious Atonement: that Jesus was God and took the burden of man's sin upon him when he died upon the cross. He also originated the idea of justification by faith. This was later interpreted to mean that if a man of evil life experienced on his death-bed a sincere conversion to faith in Christ, all his former sins would be remitted: he would suffer no penalty on account of them after he died. There is no such teaching by the Jesus of the Gospels.

Above all, Paul envisages Jesus as the great Mediator between man and God, whereas in the Gospels Jesus always pointed his followers directly to the Father. He never suggested that he must come between them and God.

To sum up, Paul's teaching about the religion of Christ was in some important respects not in accordance with the evidence of the Gospels and the teaching of the twelve apostles. What is the explanation of this?

I would suggest that it was Paul's knowledge of contemporary 'mystery religions' that unconsciously coloured the visions and revelations he claimed to have experienced. This is not a new idea. It has been put forward by a number of Bible scholars, and has been denied by others.

Paul, as we know, came from Tarsus, which was a centre of Mithraism, considered to be perhaps the chief rival of the Christian Church in its early days. Mithraism, although it originated in Persia, had close connections with other ancient mystery religions in Babylonia, Egypt and Greece.

The god Mithras became known as "a saviour, a redeemer, eternally young, Son of the Most High and preserver of mankind from the Evil One. In brief, he is a pagan Christ." (C. W. King, *The Gnostics and their Remains*, 1887.) His birthday was 25th December. He ascended to heaven in a chariot, having taken part in a ceremonial meal with his chief followers—a communion meal which became one of the most important rites of the Mithraists. The Last Judgement was presided over by Mithras, who conducted the faithful to the heavenly spheres.

In addition to the redemptive activity of the god there was his warlike aspect. He had a special regard for the military virtues of discipline and courage. Blood and sacrifice figured largely in his religion, which included the *Taurobolium*, a regenerative bath in the blood of a newly-killed bull.

Paul was an orthodox Jew, but he must have been aware of much of the teaching of Mithraism, and probably was attracted by certain of its characteristics. There was a good deal of the soldier in his make-up.

His powers of endurance and single-mindedness were military virtues which helped to make him the great pioneer missionary he was. Also, as I have said, there seems to have been a hardness or lack of sensitivity in him, which was certainly common among soldiers.

It is obvious that Paul could never have accepted the religion of Mithras. First he was a whole-hearted Jew, and after his conversion a whole-hearted Christian until his death. But is it not possible that his conception of 'Christian' included Mithraic elements which unconsciously attracted him, and which would make the new religion which he was trying to spread among the pagans more acceptable to them? They were used to the idea of a redeemer-god and the concept of his self-sacrifice in the act of redemption. Mithras was identified with the sacrificial bull in the Taurobolium.

Basically what we believe about Christianity depends upon what we think about a person. In the words of the Gospel, "What think ye of Christ?" Modern Biblical scholarship, although it has shown that some of the contents of the New Testament are of doubtful authenticity, yet reveals Jesus as a figure unique in history. It has not shown that he claimed to be the equal of the author of the universe and that he was 'very God', as the Nicene Creed puts it. On the other hand, it is difficult to see in him a man whom we can compare with any other known to us. He was like no Christian saint.

He spoke with great authority about God, his Father, and His will for mankind, which implied an intimacy of relationship with God which the saints did not claim. He exhibited none of the humility which is such an attractive feature of all the true saints, but would not be appropriate for a soul who had found the complete answer to the problem of temptation to sin.

The definition of Jesus which the Church Fathers finally agreed was a formula which the main opposing theological parties could accept. Jesus was truly God, and at the same time he was truly man: he had two natures. But this was, in fact, a contradiction in terms. As one of the authors of *The Myth of God Incarnate* put it, it is like saying a triangle is at the same time a square. The truth, it would seem, is that the relationship between Jesus and his heavenly Father is a mystery which cannot be fully understood by human theologians.

It may be of interest to note what alleged communications from 'the other side' have to say about Jesus. Some of them describe Jesus simply as a very good man whose ethical teaching has never been surpassed; whose crucifixion was a supreme example of love and nothing else, and whose resurrection was a materialisation such as has often taken place during the past hundred years or so.

But there are other communications which I find of more interest. They speak of Jesus as a soul who had travelled far among the 'many mansions' of God, but who became incarnate to found the Kingdom of God in the hearts of men and women, to enable them to find 'at-one-ment' with God. Those who sincerely tried to follow the teaching of Jesus would be helped by 'the Christ Spirit'. They would not become perfect in this world, and the wrong they did during their earthly lives would have to be faced later. Nevertheless, their bond with God would never be broken, and eventually they would be united with Him. The atonement was of cosmic significance, but beyond our present understanding.

The idea of reincarnation is often introduced. It is not generally known, perhaps, that there were Christians of the earlier centuries who had a belief in reincarnation: certainly there are verses in the Gospels which suggest that Jesus did not discourage such a belief. It took the Church more than five hundred years to decide that it was heresy.

Today, in spite of this sixth-century prohibition, I would think that there are more Christians even in the Western world who accept the idea of reincarnation than most people suppose; but undoubtedly it is in the ancient religions of the East that a widespread conviction of its reality is found. In fact, world-wide, among those of all faiths, there is little doubt that the large majority believe in reincarnation.

To consider this subject is beyond the scope of this book. A certain amount of research has been done in the last few decades; but, just as with research concerning the survival of death, different interpretations of the evidence are always possible. Proof, in the usual sense of the word, is not to be hoped for.

One thing I would say: if reincarnation is a fact, it helps to make sense of many of the problems that confront us when we try to understand the meaning of life.

The book which I found most helpful when I began to study the theory of rebirth was *The Country Beyond*, by Jane Sherwood, first published in 1944, and republished by Neville Spearman in 1969.

TEN

Tommy Porter & Abu — 'Sir Rupert Benton'

The next tape-recording session presents characters very different from Alf Higgins. Alf probably had little in the way of education, but he had that sharpness of mind which is traditionally attributed to Cockneys. Tommy Porter, the first speaker in the next tape, is a simple soul, and he was possibly what used to be called the village idiot. The ill-usage of him which he describes suggests that his earth life was at least two or three generations ago. Evidently he had been known as 'Soppy Tommy', and this is how he introduced himself to the rescue group.

The tape, of which a partial transcript is given below, was made on the occasion of Tommy's second visit. He had already been told that he had died, and he was now coming to terms with his new conditions.

The old man he mentions is Abu, the guide; and it is Abu who makes his comments on the case when Tommy goes. [In fact there has been a transposition here. Abu's comments were made after Tommy's first appearance, but it was thought appropriate by Mr. Hunt to put the recording in its present position.] 'Abu', it would seem from what was said on other occasions, is a generic name, meaning 'Father'.

It may be thought strange that Tommy should still feel himself to be lame. The suggested explanation is that disabilities in this life may at first be experienced in the next, but they will disappear when the mind has become used to the idea that bodily infirmity has no place in the new world.

There is, of course, the larger question of why there should be earthly-looking bodies in a *post-mortem* state. The answer is given that, in this first stage of the soul's journey after leaving the earth, there is a semblance of terrestrial conditions to ease the shock of the change through death.

N.H. is Norman Hunt; S. another member of the circle.

N.H. Tommy Porter!

T. *Soppy Tommy! I can talk to you now, can't I? I don't mind now any more. I'm a lot happier than I was. People are going to teach me about things now. Yes they are! I want to learn now. I didn't like people talking to me before, but I don't mind now, because they're very kind to me. So I'm going to start learning now, and see what I can do. One day I shall come and talk to you, and I won't be Soppy Tommy any more, will I?*

S. You are not Soppy Tommy now!

T. *I am a little bit still, ain't I? I know that; but I don't mind now. Yes, of course I know it. I used to be quite soppy, didn't I?*

N.H. Well, you weren't a very happy Soppy Tommy . . .

T. *I'm a happy Soppy Tommy now, and I don't mind. But they're going to teach me all sorts of things, and then I shall know properly where I am, won't I? You told me I was dead, didn't you? I ain't dead, am I? Goodbye. I'll come and talk to you again.*

That old man's just been. He looks very happy. Yes, he do! I saw him before he went away. He shook hands with me—yes, he did! He's gone. I don't know where he's gone, but I don't live with him. I've got a lady what's a-going to look after me. Yes, I have! She's a bit like my mum was—a bit. They're all very kind; so I'll go away now, but I'm coming back.

I had to be helped here, just like I used to have to be helped, because I couldn't walk very straight, I couldn't. I used to go about from side to side. When I'd got anybody with me they had to hold me straight. I'd bump into things, you know. They had to help me to come and talk to you. It's silly, isn't it? But I won't have to be helped soon. Do it by myself soon, I will.

I think you're all very kind people too, aren't you? You have been very kind to me, you have. You never called me nasty names, or throwed nothing at me, did you? Lots of people used to, but they don't now. It's going to be all right. I'm going to be ever so happy where I'm starting to live. I'm going away now. It's nice to see you people too, because I can be happy now. I'm going away . . . .

A.　　*I am Abu.*

S.　　Good evening, Abu.

A.　　*In hearty agreement with my son. It is, indeed, a wonderful thing to watch and observe the blossoming of the spirit when it is transplanted into circumstances which do not inhibit its natural growth. The joy and lightheartedness which emanate from the one who has just spoken to you is an object lesson to so many here upon the spirit side; and would be so to many upon earth could they but witness what I myself am able to see. There is a natural spirit — a spirit unspoiled by his contacts, which were unhappy and unfortunate ones in the earth world; and yet unfolding as a child, developing sweetly and naturally with love in his heart, and a joyousness which is not very usual among the earth dwellers.*

And yet one would say, reviewing his life upon earth and his unhappy and unfortunate decease, that it was a tragedy. And one would ask why should a loving God permit such a dreadful thing to occur. Here now, five minutes after his passing from earth to spirit, he is, as I say, a natural child of our Father, unfolding and developing so beautifully that it is a joy to watch. And yet people upon earth, with their so very limited vision, will still ask how can it be a loving God when we see this and that upon either hand.

It is understandable, for your vision is limited. But for one whose eyes can be opened a little—perhaps it is an act of faith; I do not know, for I can see. But you will know, my children, from what I have tried to tell you, and what so many others have endeavoured to bring to you; that the span of earth life is, by comparison, so short; so virtually unimportant by comparison again that no question of the loving kindness of God can possibly arise in your mind a little later on.

For in my Father's house are many mansions, and the scope is unlimited for each and every one of his children. Only by their own minds and their own hearts can they be circumscribed and held down, and plunged into darkness and unhappy conditions.

This object lesson of a little one, whose life upon earth was tragedy . . . and to watch him now! 'Tis pity that the education and the erudition so often educate the childlike nature out of man, which this one has retained. Be as little children in so far as you can, my dear dear ones. Your eyes must, of course, be turned to earthly things. You have affairs and matters which must be seen to, must be attended to.

But I think I need not request you or advise you to keep a corner of your heart untouched by such; with the knowledge, the certainty, that we are all children of the one Father, and that in so far as we can retain our childlike attitude, so shall we more easily and readily develop when we enter into our natural station, which is the life of the spirit. For it is easier, so much easier, for one such as this, than for the cold-hearted and yet active and keen-minded man who has bent his attention all the time upon earthly achievements — mental or material, it does not matter which. Be ye then as little children, in so far as ye may, my children; for of such is the kingdom of heaven.

Abu may sound rather pompous, or at least pedantic. I can only say what I have stressed before: that the printed word is a poor substitute for the spoken communication. Nearly all of those who have listened to Abu have been impressed by what they heard. He did not show that lofty condescension which is a characteristic of certain self-styed guides; and sometimes he exhibited a nice sense of humour.

Tommy Porter's voice and mannerisms were extremely interesting. I played the above tape to a neighbouring vicar (who is now a bishop) and his wife, who used to work professionally among the mentally impaired. I remember her being particularly impressed because she felt that Tommy sounded so exactly like her former patients that he must be who he claimed to be. Any sort of imposture seemed to her an impossibility.

The next tape includes the disclosure by Mr. Hunt to the communicator of the fact that he is dead. Another point of interest is that 'Sir Rupert Benton' claims to have died during the reign of William IV. But even if this communicator did live in the early part of the last century, he certainly was not Sir Rupert Benton.

He admitted this at a subsequent sitting, when he acknowledged that at his first appearance he had presented a facade which bore no relation to reality. He seemed deeply unhappy and remorseful, but not simply on account of his previous pretence.

Once, during a visit to Mr. Hunt, I was allowed to hear another tape, which contained a later communication from the bogus Sir Rupert. Just to listen to this recording was a harrowing experience: so pitiable an alteration had been made in the character of the man. In place of the confident, condescending nature of the first communication, there was a desperate cry from someone fleeing from two spirits who he believed were trying to destroy him.

He had confessed to Norman Hunt that in his earthly life, among other misdeeds, he had seduced and ruined a girl; and he was convinced that her brothers, who had died, were trying to avenge the wrong he had done her. Mr. Hunt tried to assure him that, far from this being the case, the two spirits in question were only trying to help him to escape from the miserable conditions to which the manner of his former life had brought him.

The outcome of this case was that a very changed 'Sir Rupert' took the first steps towards a more tolerable state of being.

In the following extract from the recording he is describing the pleasures of his earlier life.

R.B. . . . *The parson was delighted to dine with me. Sir George would give me the pleasure of his company from time to time. Lady Clarice . . . many times we have gone . . . we have gone to what was the gay city in those days. You perceive, of course, that this is many, many years ago.*

N.H. Well now, this is what I want to come down to . . .

R.B. *You do understand . . .*

N.H. What has been happening in the meantime?

R.B. *I've been . . .*

N.H. It seems a long time, doesn't it?

R.B. *Yes, a great, a great long time, and you tell me of many changes.*

N.H. Oh yes, enormous.

R.B. *I've rather been wondering myself, you know . . . to tell you the truth, and this behind my hand, the common round becomes a little wearisome.*

N.H. I'm sure it does.

R.B. *Erstwhile we were able always to amuse ourselves, as a gentleman would — and should, indeed. For always there is the quality and the lower folk; and one does not recognise the lower folk, you understand. Or, should I say, one did not in my day.*

N.H. Yes, well, it had better be put that way, I think, because there have been many changes. We've agreed on that, haven't we?

S.   May I ask if you were associated with parliamentary matters?

R.B. *Indeed no. I would have regarded such things as beneath contempt.*

S.   Would you really?

R.B. *The Court; yes, by all means; but . . . but . . . I am not a vain man, I have no pride; on the fringe only; on the fringe only: a mere equerry, a chamberlain or two, a lady-in-waiting, yes, yes, yes: but to aspire to the throne, except in deepest humility, not Sir Rupert; indeed no, not Sir Rupert; I knew my place. I trust that I upheld it worthily.*

N.H. Yes. But, as you say, looking back, all those things begin to be a little thin.

R.B.   *On the contrary, my friend; on the contrary, if you will permit me to interrupt you, without intentional rudeness, you understand. Far be that from my desire or intention, particularly in the presence of ladies; for always I have admired and respected the fair sex. But, on the contrary, in those days to which you refer, and to which I have been referring, I found life quite endurable, entirely endurable.*

It is since then that something appears to have happened. The common round, which once upon a time filled my mind and filled my requirements, now fails to do so. What is more, there are common people, quite ordinary people, you know, and they have the impertinence to rub shoulders with one. And although one can brush it away, there is always the contact—augh! But these people, they have no breeding, they have no manners, they have no dignity, and they do not understand that a gentleman of quality wishes to maintain himself in that position.

N.H. Well, you see, I'm afraid I'm going to be rather blunt. I dare say you will forgive me; at least I trust you will. I'll tell you the thing that has really happened, you see, is that no human being can live indefinitely; and you come to a time when you have to go on—somewhere.

R.B.   *Why, yes; why yes of course.*

N.H. Well, you see that time can happen — this is very strange—but it can happen without one's being aware of it.

R.B.   *No, indeed! You amaze me. Can you tell me more?*

N.H. Well, you see, we here happen to know that that is just exactly the change which you have been through without even being able to realise it.

R.B.   *Preposterous! Quite preposterous!*

N.H. Yes; but true.

R.B.   *In plain words then, my friend, you are suggesting that I am dead!*

N.H. Well, obviously, you are not dead in the usual sense. You are a very live person.

R.B.   *That, at least, should be obvious.*

N.H.   That's all that matters, you see.

R.B.   *Is it not so? It should be obvious to all concerned, including myself!*

N.H.   But there has been a change, you see.

R.B.   *A great change; a great change. A reprehensible change. I don't like it, you know.*

N.H.   That, we hope and believe, you will change your mind about. We have a great many acquaintances we have made who have passed through that change that you have just referred to as dying, which we don't really think very much of, you know.

R.B.   *Then, indeed, if I have passed through the change you have called death — and of course one is well aware that there must be a material change in such circumstances—and I haven't even noticed it; then of course one must get to the stage where one doesn't think very much of it . . . It's quite preposterous, in fact! I find it a little difficult to absorb the idea, you know. And the notion is really beyond acceptance at the moment.*

N.H.   But, you see, it can't be avoided. It can't be escaped.

S.   . . . You see, the date . . .

R.B.   *Madam, you will forgive me, but I am not aware of what you think the date happens to be.*

N.H.   Well, our date is nineteen hundred and fifty . . .

R.B.   *Oh! My dear sir, my dear sir! Hundreds and hundreds of years you are dealing with.*

N.H.   Two hundred years. A dreadful thought in a way, but . . .

R.B.   *Sailor William will no longer be there.*

N.H.   There? Where do you mean? He's where you are, you see.

R.B.   *Indeed he is not. Indeed he is not. Believe me, there are quite other monarchs who, for some reason or other, keep their thrones where I find myself now—apparently perforce—for I have no desire or wish at all to transfer my abode; but it seems to have come upon me willy-nilly, willy-nilly. And now, you see, I find myself in your withdrawing-room. I presume that is where we are; and in the association of people whom I certainly do not know. Ah!*

N.H.　That has to be explained somehow, hasn't it?

R.B.　Exactly so. Exactly so. And if one is to concede the quite preposterous proposition that I—even I, Sir Rupert— have in fact died . . .

N.H.　Yes, Sir Rupert; yet you see I'm speaking to you.

R.B.　It is to be presumed that I must be prepared to accept other equally absurd propositions from your lips.

N.H.　Well, they're very nice ones; I can assure you of that. I mean the change is a change for the better, not the worse; though it may appear so to you—you have lost so many things you were accustomed to. There are no longer quite the same pleasures that there were. But there are so many more — and finer ones. But, of course, one has to adjust oneself.

R.B.　Ah! Ah! That, I feel sure, is a word of power—to adjust oneself! It would seem to be not only a desirable, but a necessary thing. Yes, yes, I think so. Have I permission from the ladies, and from you, Sir Norman, to withdraw? I feel that this needs considerable thought.

N.H.　Will you just make one promise? And you are a man of your word, I am sure. Will you go away and think this very strange business over that I have been trying to tell you? You will find it will stand testing. It is true, in fact, in my belief. Well, we know it is true. But will you promise to come back, and have a little chat with us again if you can endure our company?

R.B.　It is most kind indeed of you to invite me again, and I would be extremely happy to accede to your kindly suggestion—always provided, of course, that I can find my way here.

N.H.　Well, somebody's been giving a helping hand, without being seen, you know. They do those things, you know, in this new kind of life you're living in.

R.B. *And have you any idea at all as to the manner in which I can find myself again among you?*

N.H. If you will in your mind ask for Sir Norman, as you have been so kind to call me, and these ladies . . .

R.B. *I may refer to my friend, Sir Norman?*

N.H. If you care to do so, I shall be quite happy. That will ensure you—I give you my word on this—that will ensure you that you will find yourself in the same situation that you are now, and you will be able to speak to us.

R.B. *A slender link, and yet it would appear to be all that there is; and so we must try it.*

N.H. Slender, like a bracelet, but strong.

R.B. *Obliged to you, sir; much obliged. You have been very kind. The ladies, my respects. Not without confidence shall I hope to find myself in your charming company. The ladies, by the way, Sir Norman, tend these days, it would seem, to speak a little more freely than in my time.*

N.H. Oh yes, indeed. That is one of the changes, you see. The ceremony and the things which were part of your life, and very naturally so; they have eased off, without, we feel, any real loss of true dignity, you know, and true sincerity and so on.

R.B. *If I let you into a little secret—the ladies may close their ears for a moment. In my day, had one been able to achieve this impossibility—to speak with one who, if your claims be true, has newly risen from the dead, the ladies would undoubtedly have been overcome with the vapours! They are apparently in a stronger mould in this latter day and age.*

N.H. They have learned many things, bless them.

R.B. *I thank you. Vastly obliged to you. As I said, when I found myself first in your withdrawing-room, it's a plaguey strange business. But I find you not unpleasant company.*

N.H. Well, that's very kind of you.

R.B. *I shall avail myself of your very kind invitation just as soon as it can be arranged. But, quite evidently, much thought first.*

N.H. Indeed, and enquiry can be made from—you will find people who are very very anxious and willing just to . . .

R.B. Not, my friend, not of the lower orders, if you please. I can speak with a gentleman, you understand.

N.H. Why not? Why not? They're there, you know. Necessarily, necessarily they're there.

R.B. Very well. I will make some investigation. I will keep hold upon the link which you have offered me, and in due course I feel reasonably sure that I shall be able to haul myself back into your presence. For the moment then; you will forgive me—I appear to have no hat that I may doff . . .

N.H. (and others) Good night. Good night.

ELEVEN

William Thompson

The last example of a rescue circle case consists of extracts from three sittings during which a miner, who gave the name of William Thompson, spoke through the medium.

A violent spasm of coughing announced his arrival. It soon became apparent that he had been trapped in a mining accident and, although he believed he was still there and alive, in fact he had died. The group did not try to convince him of this. They simply tried to console and encourage him in his plight.

On the second occasion there is a complete change of scene. William Thompson finds himself in a hospital bed, after being rescued, so he thinks, from his accident. To him, the members of the group seem to be visitors to the hospital. He is glad to see them, but somewhat puzzled, as they are not acquaintances of his.

They still do not tell him what has really happened, as they feel the shock might be harmful. They do, however, suggest that he thinks about certain old friends of his who had come to see him and, if there was anything odd about them, to question the group about it.

The third sitting provided the denouement of the story. William Thompson has followed the suggestion of the group, and has realised that the old friends who had visited him had all died. This, of course, makes him aware at last that he himself is dead—although he is very much alive in his new state.

The 'Geordie' dialect is pronounced, and impossible to reproduce in a transcript of the tape. An attempt was made to trace the pit accident which had involved the miner, but this was unsuccessful.

The rescue circle was composed of several people, but I have not particularised them.

. . . . .FIRST SITTING . . . .

W. T. (sounds of coughing)   It's a right do.

Sitter   You sound as though you've got a gradely chest.

W. T. Oh, it's coming down atop of me—right down atop of me. Oh, I canna move; I canna move.

Sitter   There is nothing on top of you.

W. T. Oh, young woman, you dinna know; you dinna know.

Sitter   Were you in an accident, old man?

W. T. Who can it be? Who can it be atalking to me?

Sitter   New friends; but friends, you know.

W. T. I'm down the mine. Who can you be talking to me?

Sitter   Don't worry about that. We're friends.

W. T. Do you know Yorkshire at all?

Sitter   Yes. I was born there.

W. T. Do you know Brighouse Main?

Sitter   Yes. Yes.

W. T. I'm a Geordie myself, not a Yorkshireman. I'm aworking down here in Brighouse Main, and the workings [have] come down.

Sitter   You're all right now, old man. You're through that now, you see.

W. T. They'll never find me.

Sitter   Oh, yes, they'll find you. We've found you. We've found you. You've found us. You've found somebody else. You know, you've come to us because we can help you.

W. T. It's no canny. It's no canny.

Sitter   No; well, there's lots of things one doesn't understand. Don't bother about that. Just talk to us a bit, you see . . .

W. T. The bloody pit props . . .

Sitter   No; they sometimes break, don't they, old man?

W. T. I canna thole it at all. I canna thole it at all.

Sitter   You can thole it. Don't go far away. Were there any of your mates with you? Any mates with you? Are you alone?

Silence

....SECOND SITTING ....

Sitter   Good evening, lad.

W.T. It's good and kind of you all to come and visit me. It's visiting day at the hospital.

Sitter   Yes. How are you feeling now?

W.T. I'm fine now. I didn't think they could find me in time, but they did. They've taken me out of it all. I'm very comfortable now in the hospital.

Sitter   Have you got a nice nurse looking after you, Bill?

W.T. It's a bonny lass . . .

Sitter   You'll soon be all right again now.

W.T. I'll be doing fine. It's good and kind of you all to come and see me. I didn't know you, eh?

Sitter   No, well you will soon. New friends are soon old friends, aren't they?

W.T. Aye . . . It were touch and go. It were touch and go. I was nearly gone, and they came along and taken me out. They put me to bed, and I'm very well, very well. Do they let people come into the hospital like this?

Sitter   Have you seen any of your old friends?

W.T. Quite a lot of old friends have been around.

Sitter   And did you notice anything particular about these friends?

W.T. (coughing) I'm still feeling a bit chesty, you know. But I'm fine now. I'll be out and about, and down the pit again.

Sitter   Well, you may not have to go down the pit again, Bill. You might get another job, you know.

W.T. Aye; they tell me I'll be all right again.

Sitter   You may not want to go down the pit. You may get another job.

Sitter   In the sunshine; good for your lungs.

Sitter   Do you want to work down the pit again?

W.T. I think I'd like to work up topside.

Sitter   You would? Well, I think you can, Bill, if you like.

W.T. There are not many jobs of that kind agoing.

Sitter   Oh, yes; but we'll see what can be done. I rather think you can get a job on the top . . . in the sunshine.

W.T. They tell me I'll be all right, you know. I'll be all right when I leave here.

Sitter   What about these friends who came to see you, Bill? Did you notice anything particular about them? Were they friends you hadn't seen for years?

W.T. Some of them were young fellows I'd near forgot.

Sitter   Have you ever thought what happened to them?

W.T. They came round to see me; all very friendly, wishing me well. They weren't allowed to stay very long. I'm no so strong yet, you know.

Sitter   Well, think about these friends, will you, Bill? And just think when you saw them last, and what happened to them, will you?

W.T. Aye, I'll think a bit.

Sitter   And then come and tell us about it next time.

W.T. I expect I shall see some more of them.

Sitter   Yes, well, you may find something come to your mind that will puzzle you.

W.T. I'm a bit puzzled anyway about a lot of things. I dinna understand how it comes about . . . you're a lot of strangers. I'm glad to see you, but you're strangers to me, to come and visit at my bedside in the hospital.

Sitter   Well, this is part of our job, Bill, and we like to do it, providing you like us to come.

W.T. Aye, there's many of them that say that. They were coming round to give me a helping hand, to see that I got on all right.

Sitter   You just try to get well again soon, and think about these friends that come to see you—not us, but the others that you haven't seen for years. And if anything puzzles you, come and ask us next time, and we'll try and make it clear to you.

W.T. These nurses; they're fine girls. They say I mustn't stay very long because I'm not strong yet, you know; not very strong. But I'm feeling a lot better than I expected.

Sitter   You're a lot better than you were last time, anyway!

W.T. I dinna think I was coming through this. I didn't know they found me. I didn't know ... I must have gone unconscious, you know. But they must have found me, I suppose. They knew I were there, and some good fellows came through and they found me and they taken me out, and I'm all right now ...

.................THIRD SITTING ....

(Laughter)

Sitter   Is it Bill?

W.T.   You'll never believe it ... You'll never believe it!

Sitter   We will, you know! What won't we believe?

W.T. I'm dead! (Laughter)

Sitter   We wondered if you knew.

W.T. You told me to think around and see what I could find a bit peculiar about these friends of mine—and it came to my mind that they were all dead! Did you know all the time?

Sitter   We knew, but we didn't like to say too much, you see, Bill; because we didn't know what your ideas of being dead were, you see; and it might have frightened you a little bit. But now that you know, and all your friends are there; well, I don't think you'll find that dead is so bad, is it?

W.T. I'm satisfied! They got me out of a mess that I don't think anybody else could have done. And they put me in a very nice place, and I'm doing fine; I told you. It's very comfortable ... And there's a bigger joke still. They're going to co-opt me onto the Committee.

Sitter   Are they really? What Committee, Bill?

W.T. They've got a committee to meet these fellows that come over like me, because some of them have a difficulty in understanding and accepting.

Sitter   You'll like that job, Bill.

W.T. I was always a good union man. I like to do what I can. And they've asked me to act as soon as I'm out of this hospital — which won't be long! I'm out of my bed already . . . I don't quite understand it all yet . . .

The rescue cases which I have quoted will probably be regarded by some readers simply as fantasies originating in the imagination of the medium, and there is no way in which this view can be positively countered. But there are certainly many people who, taking into consideration the whole body of evidence of a psychic nature concerning life after death, feel that the alleged experiences of Alf and the others have the ring of truth about them.

TWELVE

Psychical Research and
Some Personal Experiences

For those who have a serious interest in psychical study, the year 1882 was a momentous one, for it witnessed the birth of the Society for Psychical Research, usually known as the S.P.R. For almost as long as we have written records of human activity, there are accounts of events which we should now label psychic; but until the formation of the S.P.R. there had been no scientific attempt to explore and explain them.

Certain odd events in Hydesville, U.S.A., in the middle of the nineteenth century, had sparked off an intense interest in communication, by psychic means, with those who had died. This interest developed into a movement which crossed the Atlantic to England, and which was called Spiritualism. But no real research was done at this time, and credulity was rampant; although there was some excuse for this if the remarkable phenomena which were reported during this period did in fact take place.

The approach of the S.P.R. was entirely different. Its investigations showed a proper sense of caution and were carried out using the acceptably scientific methods of the day. The founders of the S.P.R., like the Spiritualists, were vitally concerned with the evidence for the survival of death; but they realised, far better than the great majority of the Spiritualists, the complexities and difficulties involved in psychical research.

As the years passed and research progressed, it became clear that often what seemed to be a communication with an after-world could be explained more plausibly in other ways, and most researchers came to the conclusion that science would never give its seal of approval to the theory of survival.

For over half the present century, the attention of researchers turned more and more towards investigation into phenomena such as telepathy, clairvoyance and precognition. These were extraordinary enough, if they did in fact occur, and research into them — and into other more recently discovered psychic phenomena—continues and expands, but during the past generation there has been a gradual resurgence of interest in the question of survival, and a good deal of research is being done in this field.

There are still some, I am sure, who do not know the difference between the S.P.R. and Spiritualism. I have met some of them. Briefly, I would illustrate this difference by saying that the average Spiritualist not only believes implicitly in all the various kinds of psychic phenomena that are reported; but in particular he is certain that the survival of death has 'cast-iron proof', as can be demonstrated by any competent medium. While, on the other hand, the average member of the S.P.R., although he may be convinced of the reality of some psychic phenomena, knows that certainty concerning matters such as life after death is not to be sought through research which deserves the description of scientific. He knows that whatever evidence there may be in this field, in favour of life beyond death, more mundane explanations are possible, however improbable some of them may seem.

The various ecclesiastical denominations have done no research of their own, in the sense of experimentation, although occasionally second-hand investigations by committee have been held. There are a few of the clergy who would call themselves Spiritualists, and about a couple of dozen who are members of the S.P.R. Incidentally, many of the S.P.R. members have various scientific qualifications, and there are a considerable number of medical doctors. The list of past Presidents of the Society is impressive, and includes nine Fellows of the Royal Society.

But, to revert to the clergy: I think a growing number of them have an interest in psychic phenomena, realising, perhaps, the implications these may have for religion. Some of these clergy, who are neither Spiritualists nor members of the S.P.R., belong to another organisation, one in which the religious implications are fully appreciated. It is called "The Churches' Fellowship for Psychical and Spiritual Studies".

Although, in general, the churches have tried to ignore psychic phenomena, and have said as little about them as possible, there have been occasions when important statements have been made. The Majority Report of Archbishop Lang's Committee, as I have remarked earlier, did not speak with as confident a voice as could have been desired; and this is not to be wondered at, considering the difficulties of the subject.

But, some twenty years earlier, a more positive and optimistic statement on behalf of the Church of England was made by a committee of the Lambeth Conference in 1920. This is what it said:—

"It is possible that we may be on the threshold of a new science, which will, by another method of approach, confirm us in the assurance of a world behind and beyond the world we see, and of something within us by which we are in contact with it. We could never presume to set a limit to the means which God may use to bring men to the realisation of spiritual life."

This could be interpreted as encouraging Christians to engage in the study of the findings of psychical research, or even to undertake research themselves.

When Lt.-Col. Reginald Lester's first wife died, he had not, I think, heard of the Majority Report, whose publication had been suppressed. But, although he was an Anglican churchman and later became a lay-reader, he had no hesitation in making a sustained and serious effort to find out whether his greatly-loved wife was still alive, albeit in another state of being. His investigation, which included many sittings with mediums, lasted four years; and by the end of that period he was convinced that there existed impressive, but little-known, evidence of the life beyond death, and communication with those in that life.

He wrote a book, *In Search of the Hereafter* (George Harrap & Co., 1952), and it aroused great interest among many people, particularly those who were professed Christians. The result of this was the formation of an interdenominational society, which was given the title, "The Churches' Fellowship for Psychical Study". The addition of the word, "Spiritual", was made later. The majority of its members were lay-people, but since the inception of the Fellowship there have always been clerical members of different denominations.

Most of the members of the Fellowship were Anglicans, and it was remarkable how many bishops there have been among them. Their number steadily increased during the earlier years of the C.F.P.S., largely due, I think, to the efforts of Col. Lester.

It must have been about fifteen years ago that, by doing a simple sum, I found that nearly half of the population of England lived in dioceses whose bishops were members of the Fellowship. Some of these bishops did not have an active interest in psychical study — bishops are much busier men than is sometimes supposed—yet the mere fact that they were members of the C.F.P.S. was significant in that they realised the importance of the subject, and the growing interest in it of the people of their dioceses.

In Col. Lester's Introduction to his second book, *Towards the Hereafter,* which was, at least in part, about the same subject, he writes about the reaction there had been to his first book. After writing about the survival of death, and how the conviction of this had helped many of his readers, he continues thus:—

> "Above all, it has taught them how to live more healthy, useful and unselfish lives, and the real meaning of brotherly love.
>
> "What has impressed me very greatly is this change of outlook of people as soon as they have obtained conviction of the truth of an after-life. I have received over a thousand letters from readers of my previous book, and it has been interesting to find that quite eighty per cent of the letters have come from those to whom this subject was entirely new,

and who have been seriously anxious to obtain fuller information. Much of this correspondence has been of a very thoughtful nature from a good cross-section of the general public; and it shows how much the average man and woman today really do want to know what happens to them after so-called death."

Sometimes Col. Lester, in connection with the evidence for the survival of death, would use the word, 'proof', and in this, of course, I could not agree with him. I greatly prefer 'conviction', the term which he used in the above extract.

The choice of the wording on a badge for the Fellowship was, in my opinion, a good one, "To Faith Add Knowledge". Spiritualists speak very little of faith, and the reason is obvious. Their knowledge of psychic matters, whether earthly or other-worldly, is for them as factual as the earth revolving around the sun. They have no doubts, and in the absence of doubt faith is superfluous.

There are others, at the opposite end of the religious spectrum — or, rather, beyond it altogether — who also feel they have no need of faith. They are the atheists, but they are in a very small minority. Most people feel that there is truth in the general claims of religion: that there is a God who is responsible for all life, and that men and women are not to be thought of simply as higher animals, as modern psychologists are wont to suggest.

But, for many, and among them the members of churches, their faith is weak, sapped by what is a misunderstanding of the findings of science. They have grown up so much under the influence of a materialistic scientific world that their minds are almost closed to possibilities of a non-material kind. For them, psychical study can be an invaluable first step towards the gaining of a conviction that man is a spiritual being in a universe governed by a good God.

And even for those who have no religious doubts, the knowledge which they may attain through psychical study can help them to come to a better understanding of their Faith. The difficulty is that this knowledge must be felt to be reliable. But if 'proof' is, as I believe, impossible, at least the cumulative weight of the evidence is very considerable, and has convinced a great number of intelligent and by no means gullible men and women that the general picture of *post-mortem* life that is drawn through information of a psychic kind is the true one.

This does not make them Spiritualists. They do not accept all that they hear or read without questioning its truth as far as they can judge—and, to be fair, this could also be said of some of those who *do* call themselves Spiritualists. They try to approach the evidence with an open, yet critical, mind. But, of course, no one is without bias. Everybody is more likely to accept as true what is in favour of his own particular views than that which is not. This must be taken into consideration by those engaged in study of a psychical kind, just as it is by those engaged in research of a less unusual nature. The result of all this is that the truth of the motto of the Fellowship appears to have been vindicated. To faith, knowledge has been added, if by 'knowledge' here is meant conviction of the truth. For many religious people their faith in itself brings this conviction, but for others evidence of a psychic nature can be invaluable and enlightening.

Soon after I joined the C.F.P.S. (which was not long after it had been founded), I became interested in psychical research of an active kind, in addition to the study of what had already been done in this field. I became the Secretary of the Psychic Phenomena Committee, and in 1974 was appointed Chairman, upon retirement from that office of Canon Pearce-Higgins.

From time to time the Committee would suggest experiments that could be carried out with the co-operation of those members of the Fellowship who were interested in taking part in research. These experiments were not necessarily directly connected with the problem of survival, but we knew that increasing knowledge of almost any psychic phenomenon could have a bearing upon it. A short description of one such experiment might be of interest.

The object of this experiment was to find evidence, if we could, of emotion playing an important part in the process of telepathy or clairvoyance, as had been suggested by other researchers. Since then a good deal of work has been done in this direction, but, when we discussed the project, the study of emotion in connection with psychic phenomena was in its infancy—in the West, at any rate.

In the *Quarterly Review of the C.F.P.S.*, I wrote that on a certain day I would place two pictures, one on the left side and the other on the right side of the table in my study at 9 a.m. On the following day, at the same time, I would change them for two other pictures, and this process would be continued for a week. I asked those who were interested to sit quietly at any time of the day or night on each of the seven days; to think of the pictures, and to draw or describe what they saw. To each of those who took part in the experiment I sent a photograph of my study table—with two blank pieces of paper upon it—so that there was some kind of link between us: as it happened, I had met none of them.

After the completion of the appointed period I received from some forty members the results of their efforts. Unfortunately I had to discard about half of them, as they had not persevered for the whole week, and their entries were not suitable for statistical analysis.

I should mention that, should the experiment prove to be successful, either telepathy or clairvoyance might be involved. In the case of telepathy, information from my mind would be received. If clairvoyance was operating, the information would be gathered from the pictures themselves, with no involvement of my mind. As, naturally, I thought about the pictures from time to time—and in any case the knowledge of them was present in my mind—it would be impossible to decide whether telepathy or clairvoyance was responsible, should the experiment prove successful.

As a matter of fact, it was. What I had not told any of the experimenters was that on the left side of the table I would place a drawing of a geometrical shape or arithmetical symbol, while on the right side I would put a picture which the Committee had felt might have an emotional appeal—such as a baby or a church spire. I had not even told the experimenters what was the object of the experiment.

After an evaluation had been made, it was found that there was evidence that telepathy or clairvoyance—or both—had been operative. What was more interesting was that extra-sensory perception—E.S.P.—appeared to be much more active in the case of the 'emotional' pictures compared with that of the others.

E.S.P. seemed to help the experimenters to get an idea of the pictures of emotional content more than it helped them to see the shapes and symbols. And when they did get some idea of the latter, there was evidence that their unconscious minds would change it into something of greater interest. For example, a triangle might appear in their conscious minds as a bunch of grapes.

It is obvious that the evaluation of the experimental material was of great importance. I need hardly say that I took no part in the process. Four people who had no interest in the experiment, and who did not realise the significance of the result of their marking, were called in to help. The method used in the evaluation of the evidence is too complicated to detail here, but later on when I described the experiment to Sir George Joy, who was at that time the Secretary of the S.P.R., he expressed his approval of the way in which it had been done, and encouraged us to continue with our research.

There are always those who shrug their shoulders and say, "Coincidence". One lady who had taken part in our experiment proved outstandingly successful in the results which she obtained. I was so impressed that I went to see her; she lived about forty miles away. She told me that a number of years earlier she had taken part in an experiment by S.P.R. researchers — an experiment involving telepathy or clairvoyance. It was only later that I learnt that not only had she taken part in it, but she had proved to be the star performer!

A good many years later, the Fellowship added the word, "Spiritual", to its title, which then became "The Churches' Fellowship for Psychical and Spiritual Studies". This was partly to emphasize that the psychic must not take too important a place in life, however interesting some members might find its phenomena. The psychic is at a lower level than the spiritual, when the latter word is defined in a religious sense. One result was that mysticism came to take a more prominent part in the activities of the Fellowship than had hitherto been the case.

In 1975 there was a new development. Some of the members of the Psychic Phenomena Committee produced a small quarterly magazine which was given the name, *The Christian Parapsychologist*. Its editor was Leslie Price, who, although a young man, had considerable knowledge of the field of psychical research (he was co-opted to the Council of the S.P.R. in 1976). The first issue of this little journal was published in September 1975, on behalf of the Committee.

The circulation was small, and although during the next year or so it increased steadily, it was obvious that without official backing the magazine would never become financially viable. Therefore we sought to make it an official publication of the Fellowship.

After much discussion this was agreed, and the journal flourished. It now has nearly three times the number of pages that it had when it began, and more than three times as much reading matter. The editor is now the Venerable Michael Perry, Archdeacon of Durham, and among the contributors to the current issue, at the time of writing, are an Anglican bishop, a Jesuit priest, and the editor of the *Journal of the Society for Psychical Research*. As its name suggests, *The Christian Parapsychologist* is concerned with those psychical phenomena which may have a bearing upon the Christian religion. This is in keeping with the Fellowship's definition of the reason for its existence—"the study of the wider reaches of the paranormal and extra-sensory perception in their relation to the Christian faith".

I have found that, generally speaking, mediums are apt to flatter their sitters. Before I met my first medium I had already read that this was so, and when he told me that some time in the future I should address large numbers of people on psychic subjects, I felt that here was a good example.

Although by that time I had been a priest for nearly twenty years, I had a definite dislike of public speaking. Among all the duties that are involved in a vicar's life, the one I really had no liking for was the preaching of sermons.

I had recently joined the Fellowship, and had been persuaded by its first Secretary, the Rev. Maurice Elliott, to form a C.F.P.S. study group. This I was willing to do, as these groups rarely numbered more than about twenty people, and anyway I usually arranged for a speaker to come to address us.

But, somehow or other, as I became better known in the Fellowship, I was asked to go to talk to other groups, and even to lecture at public meetings. To my surprise, I found no difficulty in this. I felt that I was providing information about a subject of great importance, yet about which very few people — and hardly any of the clergy — had even the smallest knowledge.

Later on I was asked to become the C.F.P.S. Regional Organizer for the West Midlands. This meant a good deal more public speaking, and I found that almost all my audiences reacted towards what I told them with considerable interest. This was not because I was a good speaker, but because of the fascination of the subject matter.

There was something, however, about which I was disappointed. Most of the people to whom I talked were middle-aged or elderly. There was usually a sprinkling of younger people, but it was rare for anybody under twenty to be present.

In 1968 the Council of the West Midland Region decided to try to do something about this, and we arranged a Youth Rally in Birmingham. Careful preparations were made, and there was adequate advertising, but the rally, numerically at least, was a failure. Little more than a handful of young people came.

I thought about this, and came to the conclusion that if youth would not come to us, we must go to them; so I set up what came to be called the Colleges and Schools Speakers Panel of the Fellowship. The response was most encouraging. During the next few years our speakers gave talks to many thousands of young people — the majority of them fifth- or sixth-formers in various types of school; but also a number of undergraduates and graduates at universities.

After three years I was able to include in the letter which I sent to headmasters and headmistresses the following statement of the Bishop of Crediton, one of the Vice-Presidents of the C.F.P.S.S.:—

"The work of the Colleges and Schools Speakers Panel of this Fellowship has already revealed that serious questions about life and its meaning are being asked by many young people today. They appear to be looking for a purpose to life, and I believe that the speakers provided by this Fellowship are giving information of considerable value, which is proving helpful in providing some of the answers to questions raised by fifth- and sixth-formers."

At the end of my letter I wrote, "The following list gives an idea of the ground which we cover in our study, and could provide titles for the talks that we can offer:— Extra-sensory perception; Apparitions and ghosts; The dangers of psychic experimentation; The problem of the survival of death; The reality of the resurrection of Christ; Parapsychology and the nature of man; Does evolution rule out divine purpose? Can psychical research support religious belief? Divine healing.

During the hundred or more talks that I gave myself, I had some unusual experiences, but for the most part my visits followed a common pattern. I would give a talk of about an hour, followed by questions. An hour is a long time for a talk in a school, but from a period of teaching in India I could tell with some accuracy when my listeners were getting bored—and it just didn't happen. The boys and girls were so absorbed in the subjects with which I and our other speakers dealt that there was hardly a sound except, hopefully, when I attempted to make a joke.

To our speakers, naturally, question time was of greater interest than their preceding talk. Questions were never lacking, which was very good. What was also good was the rarity of the hostility which might have been expected from those with certain extreme religious views. Only once was I accused of being an emissary of the devil! Proper scepticism was sometimes expressed, and that was to be welcomed. Gullibility is much more dangerous, and I always took care to emphasize this.

The majority of the visits that I made were either to comprehensive or grammar schools. But when I had an odd experience, it was usually at a public school or a college; I really don't know why.

There was one memorable evening at one of the better-known public schools. I think, perhaps, I had better not mention its name. It was a long way from where I lived, so I was invited to stay the night with the headmaster after I had given my talk to the sixth forms. After I had given the talk to the hundred or so boys, we went to dinner. It was quite a formal occasion to which a number of staff had been invited. Because of the talk, dinner was late, and it was nearly ten o'clock when it finished. We went into the drawing room for coffee, and I thought the evening would soon be over; but it was just beginning.

I had played part of the Bernard Shaw tape to the boys. Now I was asked to play extracts from other tapes, which I did. We then tried some simple E.S.P. experiments, and after I had given a short demonstration of dowsing, several of the others tried their hand at it. It was nearly one o'clock when I got to bed!

Dowsing, by the way, seems to be becoming more acceptable in certain orthodox circles than it used to be. I went once to give a talk to an agricultural college in the

Midlands. I dealt mainly with my usual psychic subjects but, quite casually, I mentioned dowsing, which has a psychic element. My chairman was the Vice-Principal of the college, and when, on behalf of the students, he thanked me after the talk, he said that he himself was a dowser and that dowsing was included in the curriculum of the college.

On another occasion, when I gave a talk at a minor public school, I gave a warning against the use of ouija boards, something that was prevalent in schools at that time, sometimes with disastrous results. I fancy that the warning was particularly needed at this school, for as the master in charge escorted me to my car he pointed to a small building and said, "That is where the boys hold their séances!"

The danger of the ouija board is chiefly of a mental or spiritual kind, but occasionally there are physical effects. As I was talking to the staff of a teacher training college about the ouija board, one of them interrupted me to say that the previous summer some of the men students had been experimenting with one when two of the windows in the room had shattered—and this had instantly discouraged their curiosity.

In 1969 I was invited to give a talk at Westcott House, the Cambridge college where graduate Anglican ordinands are trained. It so happened that in the next parish to mine the vicar was the Diocesan Director of Training for Ordinands, and I mentioned to him my impending visit to Cambridge. He was most perturbed—on my behalf—and warned me to be extremely careful in what I said there about psychic matters, or I should be in serious trouble.

I took no notice of his kindly concern, and gave my usual kind of talk. There was no unfavourable reaction whatever. Indeed, the question time gave no indication that anyone present had grave theological doubts about what I had said, or about the G.B.S. tape, part of which I had played. I had expected at least some expression of theological umbrage, but there was no sign of it. I cannot believe that a large gathering of Cambridge graduates would be afraid of airing their views, or too polite to risk embarrassing a lecturer. Perhaps most of them were struck dumb by some of the unorthodox, or at least unusual, ideas which I had expounded!

An American friend arranged a lecture tour for me in the United States in 1972. Apart from some years in India, Janet and I had had several foreign holidays in a variety of countries, but we had never had any desire to visit the U.S.A. We had probably been influenced by the picture which television gives of that great country. The picture was not an attractive one, and although we looked forward to the tour, we had certain reservations.

These proved entirely unwarranted. The people we met were charming, friendly and most hospitable. We had a wonderful time and returned for another tour the following year. The only snag was the pressure which visiting lecturers are prone to experience in America. I had heard about this, and it proved only too true.

We landed at New York at midnight, their time. There was an hour's drive to our hosts' house; and after something to eat and a chat, we got to bed at about half past two. We had had no sleep on the plane, and got up feeling not too bright. Yet my first lecture had been arranged for the same afternoon. The meeting lasted for more than three hours, by the end of which I had difficulty in keeping my eyes open. We were invited out to dinner, but had to go to bed instead.

During the twenty days of our stay in the United States we made twelve separate plane trips, besides long train and car journeys. This is nothing new for America. Their people seem full of energy and virtually tireless. Most of those whom we met had an enthusiasm for life which is rarely seen in England, and a general optimism which was very refreshing. We were fortunate in staying in private homes during our tour, and this gave us some insight into the American way of life, certain aspects of which were different from what might have been expected.

I will give just one example. We had understood that crime flourished in America a good deal more than in our own country, and that people there were very security-minded in respect of guarding their houses and possessions. Yet our first hosts, who had a lovely home filled with antique furniture and expensive electronic gadgets, told us that they never locked the house, not even when they went away on holiday. I think they felt that if a burglar was determined to get in, he would be bound to succeed, locked doors or not.

In addition to the lectures, I had many private talks with people, was interviewed by the press, and had one television interview. This was a new experience for me, and I was pleasantly surprised to find how relaxed the whole business was. I had a thirty-minute programme to myself, and sat between two interviewers whom I had met only ten minutes before, but who had quickly put me at ease. We were in what seemed to be an ordinary small room, with no sign of cameras, special lights, or other equipment.

The interview was based on the booklet I had written and which had been given my bishop's approval. It included accounts of the Grace Rosher case and direct voice mediumship, yet the interviewers gave no hint of the attitude usually found in similar psychic programmes on British television, where the interviewed person is made to feel a crank, and possibly a charlatan. My interviewers were courteous and friendly, expressed neither belief nor disbelief in what I said, and treated me as a fairly normal sort of person, which I hope I am.

Our last hosts lived in Virginia Beach, and one of our final memories of this first tour in America is the question that an elderly coloured woman, who came to clean the house, put to us. "Can you tell me," she said (I can't represent her Southern accent), "Is our President your President too?" Evidently she had the idea that Britain might well be one of the States of the U.S.A.

In December 1973 we began our second tour, this time a much more leisurely affair which lasted for five weeks, and did not entail so many talks or so much travelling. Janet began giving lectures too, not about psychic matters, but about Shakespeare's England. She had lived most of her life not far from Stratford-on-Avon, and it proved a popular subject.

Our hosts with whom we stayed for the greater part of our time in America were exceptionally kind and friendly people. We had never met them before, yet we became real friends, and I have a happy memory of Anna, at the end of our long stay when we were saying our good-byes, telling me that she looked on me as a brother.

They lived in Pasadena, a few miles from Los Angeles, which, apart from anything else, is renowned for its smog. It is said that when a post-mortem is carried out upon anyone in Los Angeles, a fairly accurate estimate of the number of years that person had lived in that city can be made from the condition of his lungs. Janet always felt ill, just from driving through it.

After we had given some local talks, we flew to San Francisco to visit a couple whom I had married in England thirty-five years earlier. We had never seen them since, but they showed us that hospitality which is so typically American.

It was during our stay with them that I went to see a professor who was a distinguished physicist at one of the leading universities, and the West's chief authority on a phenomenon in which I was at that time particularly interested. After we had finished our discussion about this, I asked him whether he could give me any information about Uri Geller, whose metal-bending exploits were making headlines at that particular time.

He told me that some of his colleagues had made an investigation of certain of Uri's activities, but he had not taken part in this. However, there was something he could tell me. One of the investigators had shown him a metal ring which they had given to Uri, and which had been fractured in their presence. He was asked to examine it under an electron microscope and, when he had done so, he found that the molecular structure of the metal had been distorted in such a way that a force must have been used which was out of all proportion to any that Uri could have exerted. I asked him what he thought about Uri Geller, and he said that, in his opinion, on occasion at least, the phenomena were genuine.

After we had returned to Pasadena, and before we came home to England, we made another journey, this time to Tucson in Arizona, where our friend, Colonel Frank Adams, lived. First we were taken to San Diego, near the Mexican border, where I was due to give a lecture. On the day before this I did two radio phone-ins, and they could hardly have been more different. The first took place in the afternoon in a tiny office-like room, with no fuss, and only one man, the presenter of the programme, present.

In the evening we went to a huge, very modern, hotel, and had the unusual experience of going up to the top of the high building in a lift made of glass, which crawled up the outside of the hotel and gave us a marvellous view of the lights of the city below. I had expected to be ushered into some sort of studio but, instead of that, we were taken into a large bar, very dimly lit and full of people drinking and talking. I gradually realised that this must be where the phone-in was going to take place, as in the gloom I became aware of a man talking into a microphone.

After a longish wait, I was called to sit opposite this man, who introduced me to my unseen listeners, as well as to the drinkers near at hand. My performance lasted an hour, interrupted of course by the inevitable commercials. I answered the phoned-in questions to the best of my ability, and must have satisfied the presenter, as he invited me to come again any time I was in San Diego. I was flattered by this, but I could not help wondering whether his invitation was caused by a difficulty in finding people to take part in his programmes, because this was the one occasion when I found American hospitality lacking. I was not expecting to be paid for my efforts, but at least they might have given us a drink! As it was, we had to pay for our own at an inflated price.

From San Diego we went by Greyhound bus to Tucson, five hundred miles away, much of this through the Arizona desert. It took about twelve hours and was quite a comfortable trip; although we were surprised at the shabbiness of the stopping-places, usually in the poorer parts of a town. It was the only time, I think, that we saw something that did not match our picture of an affluent America.

We had a most enjoyable stay with the Adams in Tucson, where I gave another couple of lectures. Before these, Frank took us to meet Susy Smith, the leader of the group to which I was going to speak. In the United States she is well-known as the most prolific writer of books on psychic subjects—by then their number had reached twenty-three — and she is psychically gifted herself. Some of her books are to be found in libraries in England. She had been known from coast to coast as a newspaper columnist, but in 1955 she had suddenly given up all her other activities to concentrate on psychical research.

We got on very well together, and after a time she showed me a copy of her latest book, *The Book of James* (Berkley Publishing Corporation, 1974), and pointed to the page which preceded the book proper. As I looked at the single paragraph which occupied the page, I saw my own name, and then realised that what was printed was an extract from a book to which I had contributed, and which had recently been published. This was *Life, Death and Psychical Research* (Rider & Co., London, 1973). It was a book which had been produced by the Psychical Phenomena Committee of the C.F.P.S.S., and the extract was taken from my chapter on the nature of life after death. The paragraph quoted ran as follows:—

> "I can conceive of no greater service to man than to provide him with a credible picture of a life beyond death; which makes sense of his striving and suffering on earth; which points to love as the principle of the universe, and which shows a progression towards ultimate union with that love which is God."

I went on, in that book, to suggest that psychical research can do this; and that is the chief reason why I have written this book.

But, of course, it would be wrong to go through this life with eyes constantly fixed upon the life to follow it. The value of our earthly experience lies mainly in human relationships here and now.

There ought to be satisfaction and joy in every life, but in every life there is certain to be trouble of one kind or another, whether it be of body, mind or spirit. It is significant, I think, that a great number of those who are most convinced about the truth of the picture of life here and hereafter which psychic evidence suggests, have a special concern for the suffering of others, and as a consequence have an active interest in healing; particularly in what is commonly called 'spiritual healing'. I should like to say something about this in the next and final chapter.

THIRTEEN

Non-Medical Healing

I first became interested in non-medical healing in 1956. I was at that time the vicar of three small parishes on the outskirts of Rugby. In one of these parishes was a three-year-old girl who had been born with a deficiency in her sight about which the doctors were able to do nothing. It was so severe that when she ran about she would knock into tables and chairs which she had been unable to see.

Her mother saw in a newspaper the announcement of a healing service to be held in a Coventry church, conducted by a Methodist minister. She took her little daughter to the service, and she was immediately and completely healed. I knew this child before and after the healing, and there was no doubt in my mind that an inexplicable cure had taken place.

I had understood before the healing that doctors had told the mother that some essential part of the optic mechanism was imperfect, and that this made any improvement impossible; so when I saw the little girl running about safely and looking with enjoyment at picture books, which she had been quite unable to do a few days earlier, I was forced to realise that something remarkable had happened.

I learnt later that the Methodist minister had first been encouraged in his healing ministry by Harry Edwards, the best-known spiritual healer in the world at that time. I wrote to Mr. Edwards to ask him if I might visit his healing centre at Shere, near Guildford, to see him at work. With his reply he sent me an 'observer ticket', which enabled me to sit within a few feet of the healer while he treated his patients.

The session lasted about two and a half hours, and there were some twenty people there hoping for help, accompanied by relatives or friends. I was immediately impressed by Harry Edwards' psychological approach to his patients—his 'bedside manner', as it were. More impressive was what seemed to be his intuitive knowledge of whatever the trouble might be, and the exact site of it, on which he would place his hand. The sceptic might say that he had been informed before-hand of the necessary medical details, and I cannot prove that this was not the case.

As I watched, about half of the patients reported a definite improvement in their condition, and nearly all of them seemed happier after Mr. Edwards had laid hands on them and expressed his confidence that healing in varying degrees would come.

All this I observed with interest from my vantage point close to the healer; but about half-way through the proceedings I received something of a shock. Mr. Edwards, whom I had not previously met, and who had not even said "Good afternoon" to me when he came in, now turned to me and invited me to lay hands, with him, on the remainder of the patients.

A little nervously I accepted his invitation, and for an hour or so we laid hands together on those who were seeking healing — my hands being placed beneath his. As before, the results seemed to vary, but there was one incident of particular interest. There limped forward a lady who had an ankle stiff and painful with, I suppose, arthritis. It seemed completely locked. Soon after I had placed my hands, under Harry Edwards', upon her ankle, I felt the ankle becoming quite supple; and in a few minutes she was able to walk, without any pain, quite normally—something she had been unable to do for a very long time.

Had her affliction been psycho-somatic? I am unable to say, but one thing seemed certain. Now she could walk comfortably, quite free from pain, whereas previously she could not. If only doctors would co-operate with non-medical healers, great advances might be made in the process of healing, both orthodox and otherwise. I know that it is extremely difficult for a doctor to co-operate with medically unqualified healers, but the position is slowly improving.

When Mr. Edwards' patients left, he asked me to stay behind, and he then informed me that I was a healer and should do something about it. I must admit that I was impressed by what he said. His reputation was such that doctors (more daring than most of their colleagues) not only sent patients to him, but sometimes even came themselves to receive treatment from him. His opinion that I had a gift of healing had to receive attention.

By this time, in my search for psychic knowledge, I had visited a number of mediums, and nearly all of them had told me that I had a healing gift—some of them seeming to believe that I was a doctor. However, from my reading of a great many books on psychic subjects, I knew that it was extremely common for mediums to credit their clients with such an ability, so I had not been particularly impressed. But Harry Edwards' statement had to be given more weight.

I thought about it, but came to the conclusion that I was not called to a healing ministry. I felt that my work, apart from that as an ordinary parish priest, lay in other directions.

Nevertheless, over the years, I have had some experience of non-medical healing, although little of it was mediated through me. In one of my parishes was an elderly woman, Mrs. A., who had suffered for years from arthritis. She had reached the stage when her hands were claw-like. She could not walk upright, and her feet were so affected that she could not wear ordinary shoes, but shuffled about in slippers. She was an eccentric character and belonged to no church, but I got to know her fairly well. I talked to her about what in religious language is usually called divine healing, and lent her books about it.

Then, one day, I had a great surprise. I met Mrs. A. and she was almost completely cured. She told me what had happened. A few days before, she had been lying awake in pain, late at night, and had switched on the radio, hoping that some music might distract her attention from her discomfort. Instead of the music she expected, there was a talk by a Christian Scientist, who described what sufferers should do to find healing. She followed his directions and was instantaneously cured.

There could be no doubt of it. Her hands were no longer like claws — they were supple and straight — and she could stand upright. Not unnaturally she was delighted, but she was not quite satisfied. Somehow or other her feet had not shared in the healing. They were still encased in the old slippers, and she still found difficulty in walking.

She asked me to arrange for her a meeting with Dorothy Kerin, a very well-known healer, about whom I had lent her a book. I found that it would take a considerable time to arrange such an appointment, and Mrs. A. was anxious that something should be done soon.

It so happened that at that time I had got together a little group of friends who met every week to pray for the sick; and I suggested that we should hold a special service in the parish church for Mrs. A. one weekday morning. I took the service, and another vicar—one of the group—laid hands on her. By the next morning her feet had been healed, and for the first time for years she was able to put on ordinary shoes and to walk normally. Her doctor was mystified by all that had happened, and could offer no explanation. There was no relapse—I knew her for several years afterwards.

I have never undertaken a study of non-medical healing and, although I have read a good many books on the subject, I am here only concerned with what I have experienced myself. From that limited experience I have found that in healing of this kind it is arthritis that is most amenable to treatment, if that is the appropriate term.

I arranged with my friend, the vicar who had been instrumental in the healing of Mrs. A., that healing services should be held in both of the parishes of which I was vicar at that time; not private services, but incorporated in an otherwise ordinary weekday evening celebration of Holy Communion. The only difference was that I used special lessons and added some prayers specially composed for the occasion. My friend spoke very simply for about five minutes, and then laid hands on those who came up for healing.

The atmosphere during the services was remarkable. After the first of them I was told by members of the congregation that the experience had been unique. This was not simply because the service had been of a type in which they had not taken part before, but chiefly because of an unusual sense of reality and purpose.

These comments of the parishioners to which I refer were made to me immediately after the services. It was only later that I learnt of any physical results. The morning after the first of these healing services I had four telephone calls from people who reported the healing either of themselves or of their relatives. And in each case it was arthritis that had been cured—instantaneously, it seemed.

From what I know of the subject, it is only a small minority of cases where healing of this immediate kind takes place. Usually it seems to be a matter of weeks or months. Unfortunately, complete physical healing of a non-pyschosomatic condition appears to be the exception rather than the rule, and nobody really knows the reason for this, although many theories have been put forward. But that healing occurs which is medically inexplicable, and which takes place after action—not always religious in a conventional sense—directed to that end, is something I certainly believe.

Instantaneous healing is unusual, but not so unusual, perhaps, as is generally thought. There was a middle-aged lady in one of my parishes who hardly ever came to church, and who was rather reserved in her manner when I visited her. Her old mother with whom she lived had a protracted illness during which I often went to see her, and it was during this period that I came to know her daughter well, and succeeded in breaking through her reserve.

One day she confided to me something which she said she ought to have told me before. She had gone to a healing service in the parish church, and had been immediately and completely cured of arthritis in her feet, something from which she had suffered for a long time, and about which her doctor had been able to do nothing. She had been in despair about her condition, which was most painful, but she had not been troubled by it at all since the evening when she had attended the service. She told me this several years after the healing had taken place!

And this was not the only case of prolonged reticence about reporting healing that I experienced. The daughter of another parishioner had been completely relieved of some back trouble of hers that had resisted doctors' attempts to alleviate it. Here again, it was only after I had come to know her mother really well that she told me about this, although it had happened a number of years before. Some people seem shy about telling of the successful results of this non-medical type of cure. I should think there must be a considerable number of those who practise divine healing who are in consequence unjustifiably disappointed by the apparent lack of healing in a physical sense, however convinced they may be of the spiritual benefits received.

Of course, most doctors are extremely doubtful about the efficacy of any unorthodox method of treatment, and it is hard to blame them for their opinion. Such treatment is completely opposed to their understanding of the process of healing. They are likely to say that the complaint had been probably of a psychosomatic nature, or that there had been a spontaneous healing such as may happen occasionally for no apparent reason in many diseases.

However, the fact remains that a large number of people say that they have been healed, and have remained healed, of complaints — sometimes organic — for which they have been unsuccessfully medically treated; and that their healing has followed the ministration of a non-medical healer, whether a clergyman or some other person.

Many cases of healing are reported from people who go to healers who make no claim that God is the direct agent of their cure. Instead of this, they may claim that those who have died are God's instruments in the curative process.

This sort of claim is strongly opposed by certain spokesmen of the churches. They may even suggest that the devil is behind these healings which take place without benefit of the clergy. But the similarity of the cases which are reported from ecclesiastical sources and other cases from different, often Spiritualistic, sources, is so striking that a common origin seems extremely probable.

It is suggested by some that the devil is so cunning that he mimics 'the real thing' for diabolic purposes of his own. He does good that evil may come—that those who are healed outside the Church may be tempted to become Spiritualists, who are followers of Satan! I have myself heard a priest-healer, specially commissioned by his bishop, express this view in no uncertain terms.

The oddest case of healing that I have experienced took place when I visited a Midland town to give a talk at a private meeting about psychical study. I had met neither the lady who had invited me to lunch before addressing the meeting, nor her doctor husband. When we began the meal, the doctor (who was a G.P.) had not returned from his rounds. When he arrived, a few minutes late, he surprised me by describing a certain pain which he had in his back, caused, so far as I can remember, by the malfunction of his kidneys.

I listened sympathetically, but I was rather puzzled that a doctor whom I did not know should talk to me as though I were a medical colleague. He knew, of course, that I was a clergyman, an Anglican vicar, although a rather eccentric one, given to psychical research, a subject in which he seemed to have no interest whatever.

If I had been surprised during lunch, I was quite amazed when, as we rose from the table, the doctor asked me to lay hands on him for healing. This was something I had never done before, except during my visit to Harry Edwards, so I certainly had no reputation as a healer. Nevertheless, I felt I had to accept the challenge. I certainly believed in divine healing: now it seemed that the time had come to put belief into practice.

The doctor led me into his surgery; then he knelt down before me, and I laid my hands upon his head, at the same time saying prayers for healing. He got up, thanked me, and went off to his work. He did not come to listen to my talk—as I said, he was not interested in the subject. But when we met again for tea, he informed me privately that the pain had gone. I never saw him again, and whether the relief was permanent I am unable to say.

Since then, particularly during hospital visiting, I have on occasion touched sick people with a healing intention, as I have felt that this was the thing for me to do, but I have not openly expressed this. Sometimes there seem to have been physical effects, but when I have taken part in 'set pieces', as it were, of this kind of healing, I have never felt at ease or confident in what I was doing, with the exception of my experience with Harry Edwards. At the church healing services which I arranged, although I officiated at them, I never laid hands on the sick.

Anyone, I believe, can be used as a channel for healing, but he must feel in tune with the methods which he uses. And there is no one, I think, who cannot be of value in a small group which meets regularly to pray for the sick. I have mentioned such a group that I once organised, and in connection with this there is one incident that is, perhaps, worth recording.

A lady wrote to us—how she had heard of our existence I don't know—and asked us to pray for her. She said that she had a lump in one of her breasts which caused her concern, as she feared it was malignant. She should, of course, have consulted her doctor, but apparently she was frightened to do this. She was added to our prayer list, and within three weeks she wrote to thank us and also to ask us not to continue with our prayers for her, as the lump had gone. A psychosomatic case? Who can tell?

This is an example of the desirability of doctors co-operating with unorthodox healers. But when they do try to co-operate, the results are not always what might be hoped.

It must be about twenty years ago that the Church of England set up an investigation into non-medical healing. The ultimate result might be described as a verdict of 'non-proven'. This was only to be expected, if the following little story provides a typical example of the methods that were employed in evaluating evidence.

A commission was set up, consisting of doctors and clergy. One of the latter was a friend of mine, and he described to me one case of alleged healing which had been considered. I understood that, some months before the commission sat, healers were notified of what it was intending to do; and they were invited to bring what they considered to be convincing cases of healing from their own experience.

Harry Edwards was one of the healers who appeared before the commission. Since he had first heard of the investigation he had been looking for cases which he thought might be received by even the most sceptical as evidence of healing. One of these cases which he presented was described to me by my friend.

A man had come to Mr. Edwards urgently seeking help. He said that he had a malignant growth in his neck. The healer felt that this might be one of the cases he was looking for, so he asked the man to go to a pathologist who would perform a biopsy to determine definitely whether cancerous tissue was present or not. Later the man returned with the pathologist's report, which confirmed that the growth was indeed a cancerous one. Harry Edwards laid hands on him, and soon afterwards there came another report from the pathologist, but this time it was to the effect that all traces of malignancy had disappeared.

Here seemed to be a convincing case, but no, there was an alternative conventional explanation. One doctor stood up and said that there was a simple solution of the seeming miracle. In the biopsy, by happy chance, the pathologist had removed all of the cancerous tissue! It seems that the poor healer cannot win, at least in the opinion of orthodoxy.

I retired towards the end of 1973 and, when we moved from Solihull to live in Canterbury a year or so later, I came to know the vicar of our parish well, partly because, like myself, he had an interest in psychical matters, and at one time had been a member of the Society for Psychical Research.

It so happened that just at this time the vicar had arranged to begin healing services in his church—the first of their kind in Canterbury. This was a courageous thing to do in a city like Canterbury, the centre of such a traditional institution as the Anglican Church; but the vicar, wisely, had secured the support of his Church Council, and was ready to go ahead with his plan.

A priest experienced in divine healing was needed, and I was able to suggest one, my old friend who had been instrumental in the healing of Mrs. A. and others in my former parishes. An invitation from the vicar was sent, and my friend made the long journey from the north of Scotland to take part in the initial healing service in the parish. Since that time, five years ago, there have been regular monthly healing services in the church, usually with the vicar himself laying hands on those who come for healing.

But there are times when someone else comes to help. In 1977, while my wife and I were staying with her cousin in Jersey, I was asked to go to see one of his friends who had recently begun a ministry of healing, and who needed advice which he thought I might be able to give her. This middle-aged housewife proved to be one of the most remarkable healers I had met, and I doubt whether I was able to give her any advice of value. I was of use in one way, however, for on my return to Canterbury I told my vicar about her, and he invited her to visit our parish.

She came and stayed for a week. During that short time she made such an impression that the vicar remarked that the parish would never be the same again.

Like mediums, healers are often accused of using their gifts, real or pretended, to feather their own nests, and there is no doubt that this sometimes happens, although not so often, I think, as their critics claim.

This accusation could not be levelled at Mrs. W., our visiting healer. She was invited to stay either with us or at the Vicarage, but she thought it would be better to go to a hotel, as people might want to come to see her privately. She paid the cost of the hotel, and all her travelling expenses from Jersey; and there was no question of her making any charge for anything that she did while she was in the parish. The reason for this was that her husband was a man of considerable wealth. [I mention this because nearly all of the healers I have known have had rather less than their share of this world's goods.]

Mrs. W. had never spoken in public before, not even to a small group. I brought her from her hotel to the church for the first service at which she was to speak, and as we sat in a back pew, waiting for people to arrive, I could not help noticing that she was extremely nervous.

But when she went up to the chancel steps and began her talk, she appeared completely confident, and held the attention of the congregation in a way that I had seldom seen before. On many occasions I have heard lay-people speak in church, and the unconventional manner in which they have talked has, more often than not, provided a pleasant contrast to the usual kind of clerical delivery, but Mrs. W. outdid them all.

She spoke with an informality and sincerity that was most endearing, and with a complete lack of that kind of piety which can be off-putting to so many people, yet with an obvious conviction of the goodness of God and His power to heal, whether in body, mind or spirit.

After the talk there was no laying-on of hands: that came later, the following Sunday, in the context of a celebration of Holy Communion. But as soon as her talk was over and the service ended, she was surrounded by people wanting to speak with her. Then she was taken off by some nuns to a private house to help a sick person there.

During the whole of her week with us, she had little time to herself: she was kept so busy in ministering to those who were ill, and there were convincing reports of remarkable healings. She did have time for an interview with a bishop— not the Archbishop — at the Vicarage. I was present, and his displeasure and suspicion of her activities were obvious. She did not fit into the orthodox pattern of ecclesiastical behaviour, and the reports of healing which had been effected through her were brushed aside.

The vicar himself had certain reservations about what Mrs. W. felt concerning the origin of the healing process, although he had no doubt about the beneficial results among his parishioners. The healer had told us that she believed that an ancestor of her husband on his mother's side — Robert Wright, a surgeon who had died nearly two hundred years ago—helped her in her healing. Nothing of this, of course, had been told to the bishop: otherwise his attitude, no doubt, would have been even more unenthusiastic than it was.

The vicar found the idea distasteful, and he was able to convince Mrs. W. during her visit that her belief was untrue; that it was dangerous to have anything to do with those who had died; and that, in any case, evil spirits might well be responsible for these alleged communications. She became more conventional in her attitude towards healing—accepting that it came direct from God, whereas previously she had thought of God using Robert Wright as a kind of intermediary in her ministry. Mrs. W.'s conversion to orthodoxy lasted for some time, and she was confirmed to become a full member of the Church of England. However, about two years later, she told me that she had reverted to her former conviction that Robert was helping her in all that she did to help others —but that ultimately the healing came from God.

The theory that doctors who have died may, as it were, carry on with their former careers is by no means a new one. Harry Edwards, for example, believed that healing came through him in this way, although I am not sure that he had any personal and direct evidence of this.

But there is the case of another healer where there is evidence of a quite remarkable kind. While I was talking privately to a visitor who had just given a talk to a study group of mine, he told me about a former Aylesbury fireman whose healing career he had been able to follow from its beginning. At this time the healer, George Chapman, had begun to achieve something of a reputation, but nothing like the one that became his in later years.

I was told by my informant that Mr. Chapman entered into trance after breakfast every day—every working day, I presume—and remained in trance for several hours, during which time he was visited by those who were seeking healing. This in itself was unusual enough, but there was much more to come. When George Chapman was in trance his personality underwent an impressive change. The new person called himself William Lang, and was convinced that he was a surgeon of that name, an ophthalmic consultant, who had died in 1937. This was not an alleged case of reincarnation, as Chapman was already a teenager when the surgeon died.

What was claimed was that William Lang every day took over Chapman's body, so to speak, to continue his healing work. I arranged an appointment with George Chapman, and spent some time with him when he was in trance. I did not go as a patient, but just to meet and to talk with someone about whom I had a lively curiosity. I found the meeting quite fascinating. Although Chapman at that time was only approaching middle age, the man I talked with had the appearance, voice and mannerisms of an elderly doctor of a generation earlier. He was obviously a cultured man with an extensive vocabulary, whereas Chapman could not truthfully be so described when he was in his normal state of consciousness.

But it was not this seeming change of personality in trance that had aroused my curiosity. What had particularly intrigued me was that the man who had told me about Chapman, and who knew him well, had informed me in confidence that a number of William Lang's former colleagues recognised him in George Chapman when the latter was in trance, and would meet him regularly in London. Sometimes they would even bring their patients for consultation and treatment. [I am breaking no confidence in writing this now, for it has been generally known for a number of years.]

There is little similarity between this case and that of Mrs. W. No change in her personality is apparent when healing takes place. She does not use correct medical terminology as does 'William Lang'. In her presence one is not confronted by a deceased doctor, but by a woman who simply believes that all healing comes from God, although unseen helpers may play their part.

About five years ago I formed in Canterbury a small group, composed of four Anglican priests and two lay-people, to discuss psychical matters in which we were all interested. For a year or so we considered various psychical phenomena, in particular those which provided evidence for the continuance of life after death. Then I suggested that we might try to interest as many clergy as possible in the diocese of Canterbury in what we were convinced was a very important subject. We talked over this project, and the general opinion was that the great majority of the parish clergy of the diocese would not be sufficiently open-minded to consider what we should tell them.

I therefore suggested an amendment to my original idea, namely that we should start with a project that would have a better chance of success—the production and publication of a pamphlet about divine healing, a subject in which we all had an interest and a certain amount of experience.

My suggestion was accepted, and the question then was how the necessary statement on healing was to be prepared. Although we all knew something about divine healing, none of us had extensive experience of it, but it so happened that, not long before, I had come into contact with the vicar of a parish not far from Canterbury, who had had thirty years of experience of this kind. I had first met him when he had asked me for advice about a psychic problem in his parish.

With the approval of the group, I asked him if he would help us. He said he would be very pleased to do so, and soon we received from him a statement of his thoughts about the subject, illustrated by some of his experiences. He had agreed that we might make what alterations or omissions we felt to be necessary—which later on he would be asked to approve— and we set to work.

His paper was much too long for our purpose, and also certain changes appeared to be desirable. For a year we met regularly, going over the document word by word, to produce the kind of pamphlet which we had intended, and finally we completed our task.

During this time another member of the group had made the suggestion that it would be extremely helpful if the Archbishop of Canterbury were to write an introduction to the pamphlet. I doubted very much whether he would do this, and was afraid that our efforts in this direction would involve a lengthy postponement of the publication date, due to ecclesiastical bureaucracy.

Fortunately, however, I was overruled, and the Archbishop proved only too willing to do what we asked. There were some difficulties and delays—not in any way the fault of the Archbishop, but due to the illness of his chaplain and the loss of an important letter by the Post Office—but finally we had the pamphlet, *The Churches' Ministry of Healing*, printed and sent out to all the incumbents of the diocese, buttressed by the support of the Archbishop, Donald Coggan, who himself had a very real interest in divine healing.

Clergy who were interested were encouraged to write to us, and our hope was that in this way some sort of diocesan organisation could be formed. It turned out that several clergy in the diocese were already practising divine healing, and a number of others wanted to know more about it. In 1979 an official Diocesan organisation was formed, and in March 1980 its first conference was held.

Earlier in this chapter I mentioned that, although it is difficult for doctors to co-operate with spiritual healers, the position is improving. An important step forward was made in 1978. This is described in *Notes for the Guidance of Healers*, published by the British Alliance of Healing Associations.

In the section headed, "Relationship with the Medical Profession", is the following passage:—

"Increased co-operation with doctors has been facilitated by the statement of the Deputy Registrar of the General Medical Council on 6th March 1978, that the President of the G.M.C. 'can see no reason why a doctor should not, if he considers that it would be helpful to one of his patients, either suggest or agree to a patient seeking assistance from a member of the British Alliance of Healing Associations, provided that the doctor himself continued to give, and to remain responsible for, whatever medical treatment he considered necessary for the patient.'

"Healers should always strive for good relations, and if possible, co-operation with doctors. A vital factor in building and maintaining satisfactory relationships is that healers should recognise and respect the respective rôles of doctor and healer. Healers are essentially channels for the flow of spiritual forces: they are not qualified to give medical advice or to interfere in any way between doctor and patient. Healing is in no sense an alternative to orthodox medical treatment; it is complementary to it."

It may not be generally known that there are several thousands of healers outside the ministry of the orthodox churches. Dr. Alec Forbes has put the number at twenty thousand. It would be true to say that many of them are Spiritualists. It would also be true to say that many of them are not.

Among the various healing organisations, two of the better-known are the National Federation of Spiritual Healers and the British Alliance of Healing Associations. Recently a measure of unity has been brought into the healing field by the formation in 1981 of the Confederation of Healing Organisations, which embraces most of the healing organisations in the United Kingdom.

The phenomena of non-medical healing, especially when they are obviously not of a psychosomatic nature, are so remarkable and inexplicable in terms of present medical knowledge, that it is not surprising that most doctors still regard them with suspicion.

Anything at odds with orthodoxy in any field of knowledge has its battles to fight before its worth becomes generally recognised. And this certainly applies to the main subject of this book. Some people will feel that the evidence of psychical research is so strange that it is all beyond belief. To them I would say that sometimes I feel that this very universe in which we all find ourselves is itself beyond belief; and yet we do—we have to—believe in it.

But, it may be said, is this universe so strange, so improbable? A group of galaxies has recently been discovered which are ten thousand million light years distant; and a light year is not a measure of time, but is the distance that light travels in a year at the rate of approximately one hundred and eighty-six thousand miles a second; that is, about six million million miles. Multiply that by ten thousand million, and those galaxies are seen to be sixty thousand million million million miles distant from us. Moreover, we are told that there are other more distant objects—not galaxies, but quasars—which have been detected, all of them receding from us at a tremendous velocity.

Indeed, so far as we know, there is no end to the universe. We cannot imagine this. Nor can we imagine the universe being limited. One or the other, presumably, must be true. We live in mystery, perched upon a sphere — our earth — revolving at great speed as it circles the sun; itself a speck in a galaxy of millions of suns among millions of other galaxies. Who can fathom the mysteries of the material universe? But the immaterial mysteries of life, of mind, and of spirit, are far greater.

How we interpret them, each man or woman must make up his own mind. What religious evidence—whether from the Bible, from other books, or from personal experience—we can accept, each has to determine for himself. And so it is with the evidence of psychical research. To reject all of its findings, and even its unproved theories, is foolish. To accept them uncritically is no better. To study them, I would suggest, is most desirable.

Such a study may help us to make sense of life, and what could be more important than that? It may help us to come to a conviction that our present life is but an episode in a great adventure which all mankind shares: which leads from the uncertainties and vicissitudes of mortality to a path beyond, which will lead us ultimately—in company with those we most love—to God.

Bibliography

ANONYMOUS — *The Boy Who Saw True*
Neville Spearman 1953

BARHAM, Allan — *Strange to Relate*
New Horizon 1980

FLINT, Leslie — *Voices in the Dark*
Macmillan 1971

GREAVES, Helen — *Testimony of Light*
The World Fellowship Press 1969

HAMMOND, Sally — *We Are All Healers*
Turnstone Books 1973

JOHNSON, Raynor — *The Imprisoned Splendour*
Hodder & Stoughton 1953

LESTER, Reginald — *In Search of the Hereafter*
George Harrap 1952

PEARCE-HIGGINS, John & WHITBY, Stanley, Editors — *Life, Death and Psychical Research*
Rider & Co. 1973

ROSHER, Grace — *Beyond the Horizon*
James Clarke & Co. 1961

SHERWOOD, Jane — *The Country Beyond*
Neville Spearman 1969

SHERWOOD, Jane — *Post-Mortem Journal*
Neville Spearman 1964

SMITH, Susy — *The Book of James*
Berkley Publishing Corp. 1974